DAWN FELICE WALKER

From MOTHERS *to* DAUGHTERS

Let's Talk about Sex

Published by: God's Girl Dawn
Copyright © 2024 by Dawn Felice Walker

Cataloging data is on file with the Library of Congress
LOC Control Number: 2024920995
ISBN 979-8-218-47719-6

All rights reserved. No part of this book may be reproduced in any form or by any electronic or mechanical means, including information storage and retrieval systems, without permission in writing from the author. The only exception is by a reviewer, who may quote short excerpts in a review.

Unless otherwise indicated, all scripture quotations, are taken from the King James Version of the Holy Bible.

Printed in the United States of America
Dawn Felice Walker
Visit my website at:
www.frommotherstodaughters.com
www.shesaberean.com
Email: Dawnwalker55@myyahoo.com

This is dedicated to my beautiful daughters, Jasmine, Nadia, Courtney, and my sweet granddaughters.

Trust in the LORD with all your heart, and lean not on your own understanding; in all your ways acknowledge Him, and He will make your paths straight (Proverbs 3:5-6)

I am always on your side.

I love you.

ACKNOWLEDGMENTS

All honor and praise to the only true and living God, my Father, and the Lord Jesus Christ.

To my loving husband, Paul: Thank you for allowing me the freedom to write this book and for letting me know when it was time to stop. Marriage after 50, we got this, babe. Love you!

To my mother: Thank you for your constant prayers, wisdom, and wittiness. I love you.

Tina Smith: Thank you for your sound advice, listening ear, and hours of research about everything! You are my dearest friend!

Yvette Ellis: Thank you for always pushing, praying, and encouraging me. You are my forever sister and my forever friend.

Tamara Rochelle: God made you wonderfully brilliant, and I am blessed to call you my sister-friend. Sisters in Christ, Friends for Life!

Regina Alleyne: Thank you for encouraging me to write every day. Love you.

Thank you to my Titus 2 women and all those who have loved, supported, encouraged, and prayed for me.

From MOTHERS *to* DAUGHTERS

Let's Talk about Sex

DAWN FELICE WALKER

Contents

Preface 7

Introduction 11

Chapter 1. Boyfriend's, Boo's, and Bae's 18
Chapter 2. Do You Remember Your First Time? 25
Chapter 3. Lieth at the Door 35
Chapter 4. Let's Talk about Sex 42
Chapter 5. Vows, Covenants and Curses 59
Chapter 6. Let the Healing Begin 68
Chapter 7. Learning to Forgive 78
Chapter 8. Closing the Doors 84
Chapter 9. Living Free 106
Chapter 10. Final Thoughts 121

References 125

PREFACE

Ugly! If there were one word to describe what I saw that day, ugly would be it.

God had just shone His light on one of the darkest areas of my past: my sexual past. Up to this moment, I had chosen not to look at my past because, well, then I would have had to look at it—and who wants to do that? As I saw it, this part of my life was over, so there was no need to bring up my past indiscretions. So, I did what any blood-bought, born-again believer does: I tucked this area away neatly under the blood of Jesus, gave God praise, and vowed never to discuss the dirty details, ever!

But this day, it was as if God was saying, "Daughter, I need you to see this." And then He turned on His heavenly light, and I could see… everything! I saw how my sexually immoral past had blatantly violated the commands of God. I saw how my desire for love and acceptance had led to a string of unhealthy relationships, emotional trauma, heartbreak, and even financial instability. Did I mention the light was bright?

For the first time, I saw my sins as God saw them, and the weight of it brought me to my knees. So, as I sat drowning in a pool of tears and shame, I bowed my head and repented.

This began my journey to being healed from the inside out. But it was not an easy process. I had to be painfully honest with myself and take responsibility for my past decisions, behaviors, and consequences. But as difficult as that was, I am grateful, because this process restored me and freed me from the bondages that once plagued my life.

Daughter, I want to encourage you that God knows where you are on your life's journey. He is aware of the decisions you have made thus far and the ones you have yet to make, good and bad alike. But be confident of this: no matter how wretched your past, God loves you, and He alone has the power to turn your brokenness into something beautiful.

If you have been involved in sexual immorality in the past or present, or are making plans to in the future, there's no doubt it already has or will have a traumatic effect on your life. But take heart: you can overcome it!

Please know that the material in this book is not meant to condemn you or make you feel guilty about your past (or even your present). My purpose in sharing my journey is to present the truth that makes us free and reconciles us to God our Father.

I pray that as you read through the pages of this book (along with your Bible), God will lovingly shine His light from heaven and expose all the dark places in your life that need to be uncovered. As we dig through the specific details of sexual sin, we will understand how it destroys us physically, mentally, and spiritually, and separates us from God and our God-given purpose. I pray that God will open your heart, unveil your eyes, and unplug your ears to receive the truth and reject the lies of the enemy so that you too can find restoration, forgiveness, and healing from your sexual past.

FOREWORD

As a pastor, I am often approached with questions about life, love, and relationships. One of the most frequent and deeply personal topics that arise is the subject of sex. In our modern society, the language surrounding sex has been perverted and even politicized, leaving many misguided and confused.

I am honored to support Dawn Walker in this necessary work to provide a biblical perspective on sex. Dawn has been a forerunner in ministry over the past two decades. I have had the privilege of witnessing her teach and communicate with excellence. A multi-talented gift to the body of Christ, Dawn has consistently and diligently answered the call to be a voice crying out in the wilderness. Her desire to rightly define and expound on the topic of sex is greatly needed today.

Sex is a gift from God, designed by Him to be enjoyed within the sacred covenant of marriage, and is a full expression of love, profound intimacy, and unity between a husband and wife. Unfortunately, in today's world, this divine intention is often overshadowed by societal pressures, misconceptions, and distorted representations. This book aims to reclaim the beauty and sanctity of sex as originally intended by our Creator.

I pray that as you read this book, you will find not only answers to your questions but also a deeper understanding of God's incredible gift of sex. May it inspire you to embrace His teachings, enrich your relationships, and experience the fullness of His love in every aspect of your life.

Pastor Yaves Ellis

INTRODUCTION

Let me start with this: when it comes to making important decisions about love, marriage, and sex, where do you go to find your source of truth? Why do I ask? Because everyone has a belief system or a worldview. What you believe determines how you behave, and your behavior determines your life's outcome. So, if you look at your place in life right now, your beliefs influenced the decisions that got you there.

With that, what are your thoughts about sex? Do you believe it should only be reserved for marriage, or do you think it's okay to have sex without being married?

What if I told you that sex before marriage can change the course of your life—and not for the better. I could provide a list of statistics on how sex before marriage:

* Increases the chance of divorce
* Increases the risk of emotional and physical trauma
* Increases the chance of unwanted pregnancy
* Increases the chance of STDs (sexually transmitted diseases)

I could do this, but this is not new information. Most people know there are risks to having unprotected sex, and we don't have to look far to see the evidence of unwanted pregnancies, divorce, and physical and emotional trauma stemming from such behavior in our world today.

What's society's answer? Practice safe sex. But what is safe sex? And what makes it unsafe? Seemingly, using condoms, contraceptives, or abortion is what protects you or makes sex secure. But all are temporary fixes that mask a much deeper problem. You see, what most people don't know is that the effects of premarital sex extend beyond what we see in the natural and reach into a realm we cannot see.

Let me present it to you like this: We all live in this physical world and are born into a physical family we see and interact with daily. However, there is also a spiritual realm with spiritual families that we cannot see, and you belong to one of these families.

These two families are in complete opposition to each other. Each of these spiritual families has its own worldview and systems of operation. One family represents light, truth, and righteousness, while the other represents darkness, lies, and unrighteousness.

It started with Lucifer (the devil), an anointed cherub of God, who was so taken in by his beauty that he decided, by his own power, to exalt himself above God in a vain attempt to be *like* God. This resulted in Lucifer being hurled out of heaven together with his rebel angels, and becoming the source of all evil in the world (Isaiah 14:12-15; Ezekiel 28:15). Now, his dark family, consisting of fallen angels and human beings who oppose God, fights against God's family.

However, since the devil is a created being, he can only imitate the true Creator. So, everything that God has established as good, the devil presents a distorted version of it that is as perverted as he is. God's kingdom is righteous (right side up). The devil's kingdom is unrighteous (upside down).

The devil has infiltrated the world system and overturned values that were once upheld as godly. Sexual purity, for example, is under attack as the world system celebrates promiscuity and free love. But the family of Light operates under God the Father's authority and does not adhere to this world's system. The children in God's family do not live to please the flesh but crucify it (Galatians 5:24). On the other hand, the family of Darkness operates under the influence of the father of lies, the devil, who is the prince of this world's system (2 Corinthians 4:4). The children in his family live to satisfy every lustful and fleshly desire (Galatians 5:22-23).

So do not be deceived; not everybody is a child of God, even if they claim to be. Only those who profess Christ and practice righteousness (or live rightly as instructed by the Bible) are God's children. Those who practice sin and unrighteousness are children of the devil.

1 John 3:7-10

Little children let no man deceive you: he that doeth righteousness is righteous, even as he (God) is righteous. He that committeth sin is of the devil; for the devil sinneth from the beginning. For this purpose, the Son of God was manifested, that he might destroy the works of the devil. Whosoever is born of God doth not commit sin, for his seed remaineth in him: and he cannot sin, because he is born of God. In this the children of God are manifest, and the children of the devil: whosoever doeth not righteousness is not of God, neither he that loveth not his brother.

So here is the truth: there is a battle for your mind, body, and soul—a battle for your worship and allegiance. Why? Because the devil hates God, but since he cannot attack God, he attacks His creation.

This battle began in the Garden of Eden when Adam disobeyed God's command not to eat the fruit of the Tree of Knowledge of Good and Evil. When Adam sinned, he lost his spiritual connection with God, and every generation after Adam was born into darkness, marred by the stain of sin. Our identity and purpose were also lost, which explains why we go on a mad quest to find some sense of purpose or place in the world.

The devil knew that if you were ever exposed to the kingdom of light, you would be reconciled to God through Jesus Christ, who would then begin the process of restoring your identity as a child of God, created in His image. Therefore, you would no longer have to look for purpose because you would know it through your identity in Christ.

2 Corinthians 4:3-4

But if our gospel be hid, it is hidden to them that are lost: in whom the god of this world hath blinded the minds of them which believe not, lest the light of the glorious gospel of Christ, who is the image of God, should shine unto them.

So, the main purpose of the family of darkness is to keep you from ever reaching a place where you can be remade in God's image. Satan, therefore, works diligently to keep you in darkness because once your eyes are opened to the light of the gospel of Jesus Christ, you come to know your identity. This is why Christ came to destroy the works of the devil and restore us to God the Father (1 John 3:8).

It's only when we recognize that we need to be rescued from darkness that the blinders are removed, and we are reconnected to God by His Spirit. This enables us to both see and understand the spiritual family of God.

Choose Your Family

When Jesus was approached by a man named Nicodemus, who wanted to know more about Him, He stressed the need for him to be born again: *"Verily, verily, I say unto thee, Except a man be born again, he cannot see the kingdom of God"* (John 3:3).

What is being born again? It means to be born from above—a spiritual rebirth that happens when we believe in Jesus as our Savior.

We are physically born into this world with a sinful nature (as rebels against God), and we live, act, and think in violation of God's commands. Once we realize that the judgment for our rebellion (sin) is death (Romans 6:23), we can choose death, or we can choose eternal life given to us by belief in Jesus Christ.

Our decision to believe in Jesus Christ as our Savior moves us out of the family of darkness into God's family of light (Colossians 1:12-14). This is how we become born again: we were born into sin, but now we are born again (spiritually) into eternal life. This can only be done by belief in Jesus Christ, by faith alone—not by anything you have done or can do to earn it. It is a gift (Ephesians 2:8).

Now for the record, all roads do NOT lead to God, as many religions teach. This is a lie the enemy has perpetrated for centuries to keep people comfortable in their darkness, unable to grasp the truth that Jesus is the only way back to the true and living God. In John 14:6, Jesus says, "*I am the way, the truth, and the life: no man cometh unto the Father, but by me.*"

Therefore, the only way to see the kingdom of God is by being born again, which is spiritual. Through belief in Jesus Christ, we pass from death to life, out of one family into another, from an old creation to a new creation in Christ.

This is the Gospel of Jesus Christ. He reclaims and restores what was lost; He heals the brokenhearted and delivers us from the clutch of sin and death. He makes us free.

"What does any of this have to do with sex?" you ask. My answer is that sex is an act of worship, and what you believe determines how you worship with your body and indicates who you are giving your worship to. Although many people think sex is only physical, the act of sexual union breaches the barrier between the physical and the spiritual realm, exposing us to grave spiritual and even eternal consequences.

Apostle Paul issued a stern warning against all who violate God's command regarding sexual sin:

> *Know ye not that the unrighteous shall not inherit the kingdom of God? Be not deceived: neither fornicators, nor idolaters, nor adulterers, nor effeminate, nor abusers of themselves with mankind Nor thieves, nor covetous nor drunkards, nor revilers, nor extortioners, shall inherit the kingdom of God* (1 Corinthians 6:9).

In other words, your eternal salvation can be forfeited because of sexual immorality. Why? Because whoever you yield your will and your body to is the one you pledge your allegiance to. How you worship determines who you worship, whether it is the true and living God or the devil.

> *Do you not know that if you present yourselves to anyone as obedient slaves, you are slaves of the one whom you obey, either of sin, which leads to death, or of obedience, which leads to righteousness?* (Romans 6:16 ESV)

I can say with confidence that the family you have chosen to belong to will determine whether you overcome sexual immorality or continue to be a slave to it. Notice I said "the family you have chosen," because remember, what you believe influences your decisions. So, living righteously is a choice, just as living in sin is a choice.

Therefore, I can show you the ins and outs of sexual immorality and all the chaos it will bring into your life. But if you don't believe the first truth—that Christ died, was buried, and resurrected to take the penalty of sin and death for sinners such as you and me, then none of this will matter.

For God's word to work for you, you must be a believer and follow His instructions. You must choose a family; you must choose a side. But know that your decision will have consequences: one family leads to life, the other leads to death. The experiences and principles that I will be sharing from here on will be grounded in the truth which is the word of God—the Holy Bible. So please search the scriptures provided, and do your research so that you can know for certain which spiritual family you have pledged your allegiance to.

Consider this as we journey through the rest of this book: having a positive attitude is good, making positive confessions is good, and even abstaining from sexual immorality is good, but none of these things will save you. Indeed, you must be born again.

That being said, let's talk about sex.

Chapter 1
BOYFRIEND'S, BOO'S, AND BAE'S

"Will you be my girlfriend?"

It was finally the moment I'd been waiting for my whole elementary school life. I was so excited that I immediately blurted out, "Yes!" His name was Tim, and he was my first boyfriend. Again, I was only in elementary school, but having a boyfriend made me feel special.

Since we were too young to talk on the phone, I would have to wait for school the next day before I could see him again. Even then, most of our conversations consisted of passing notes at recess. I still remember the silver heart-shaped necklace he gave me for Valentine's Day, which I only wore at school but hid under the living room chair when I got home so that my mom wouldn't find it (I may have thought having a boyfriend was a good idea, but my mom was having none of it). Interestingly, my mom seemed to be the only person against me having a boyfriend because she said I wasn't old enough. But everything else around me—culture, movies, and even adults—seemed to think that having a boyfriend was a normal part of growing up.

I had no idea what it meant to have a boyfriend, but even as a teen, I can remember being asked, mostly by adults, if I had one. I'm sure they meant no harm, but at the same time, I don't recall anyone ever asking me if I wanted to be a wife or encouraging me in that direction. No one even explained what I was supposed to do with a boyfriend. But I wanted one. And with so much focus on having a boyfriend, I made that my goal.

So, what is a boyfriend? Seriously, have you ever really given any thought to what it means?

Boyfriend: a male friend or frequent or regular male companion in a romantic or sexual relationship.

This definition implies that there is a relationship that involves frequent or regular romance or sex with a male friend. (Then why not call him a man-friend?) Now, in my case, I was not thinking about anything sexual—after all, I was in elementary school. And I couldn't get married in elementary or even high school, so what was the purpose of having a boyfriend?

Just a thought: during our adolescent years, we are emotionally unstable, lack identity, and are easily influenced. This is why we do the next generation of sons and daughters an injustice when we allow them to have boyfriend/girlfriend relationships during their developmental years. It only sets them up for heartbreak, damaged emotions, and trust issues that can linger into adulthood.

I did not realize it then, but as I got older, the concept of having a boyfriend distanced my thoughts of marriage. Instead, it created a cycle of practicing sin, specifically sexual sin. You see, the longer we stay "boo'd up," the greater the chance of getting involved sexually. Then, once we have given ourselves away sexually, we become emotionally invested, which makes it difficult for us to walk away, even from bad relationships. So, instead of allowing ourselves to be courted with the intent of marriage, we continue in relationships we know aren't God-ordained, having sex and settling for the title of being someone's girlfriend—or worse, their Baby's Momma.

This is what I call "wasting your wife," meaning you are allowing all the resources God gave you to be a wife to be wasted away on boyfriends, boos, and baes. Instead of protecting and perfecting your wife-related skills while waiting for your husband, you settle for who you can get right now. Let's be honest: we know, going into most relationships, they're not going to work. Yet we allow our time and bodies to be wasted, only to end up heartbroken and alone from a relationship we knew wouldn't work in the first place.

The End Goal

So, what's a girl to do without a boyfriend? That depends on you. Are you content with being someone's girlfriend, boo, bae, jump-off, or side piece? Are you okay with continuing to give your heart and body away? Because God created you for so much more:

> *And the LORD God said, It is not good that the man should be alone; I will make him an help meet for him* (Genesis 2:18).

God's plan for us was always to be in a place where we are loved, cherished, and protected. He never intended for us to be in a relationship where we were just someone's pastime. That is why Boyfriends, Boo's, and Baes were never part of God's plan for you.

When God created the woman, He brought her to Adam, who recognized immediately that she was a part of him, and he took her as his wife, not his girlfriend(of course, she was his only choice, but she had been designed specifically for him.

> *And the LORD God caused a deep sleep to fall upon Adam, and he slept: and he took one of his ribs, and closed up the flesh instead thereof; And the rib, which the LORD God had taken from man, made he a woman, and brought her unto the man. And Adam said, This is now bone of my bones, and flesh of my flesh: she shall be called Woman, because she was taken out of Man. Therefore shall a man leave his father and his mother, and shall cleave unto his wife: and they shall be one flesh* (Genesis 2:21-24).

And so it is that God has designed you to be the perfect fit for a certain man. Serial dating and multiple boyfriends can cause you to get off course, become distracted, and waste time—not to mention the emotional trauma that can occur with every breakup, making you distrustful in future relationships.

Even in traditional Jewish culture, having a boyfriend was unheard of. Young men and women were prepared in their youth for marriage through a contract arranged by their parents. In fact, the betrothal period was just as binding as marriage, so neither the woman nor the man dated other people. In Genesis Chapter 24, we see such a contract.

Abraham instructs one of his servants to find a wife for his son, Isaac, from among his kinsmen (which was common in those days) in a distant country. When his servant arrived at the town, it so happened (because he had prayed to God to direct him to the right woman) that he met Rebekah, the daughter of Abraham's brother, Bethuel. I encourage you to read the full chapter of Genesis 24 to understand what transpired here. But in summary, when all the details of her prospective husband were disclosed, Rebekah willingly decided to go with Abraham's servant to become Isaac's wife.

Please notice that she had never set her eyes on Isaac, nor was she going to meet him so they could date. She was chosen specifically to be his wife, and she was going back with Abraham's servant for that purpose.

Also, notice how her family celebrated this decision of hers:

> *And they blessed Rebekah, and said unto her, Thou art our sister, be thou the mother of thousands of millions, and let thy seed possess the gate of those which hate them* (Genesis 24:60).

Her family knew she was going away to become a wife, and what do they do? They pronounce blessings over her life. They affirm her role as wife and mother, and it is celebrated.

In our culture, we are often discouraged from motherhood and encouraged to date casually while we pursue college and follow our ambitions. While there is nothing wrong with pursuing education and career, we should prioritize the will of our Creator over our desires and the ways of our culture.

God designed marriage so we could find fulfillment in the roles He assigned to us and our spouses. I'm not saying everything is perfect in marriage, but I am saying that when you seek to honor God by doing things His way—saving sex for marriage and choosing to date with a purpose—you can avoid a lot of unnecessary problems. To be clear, I am not suggesting jumping right into marriage either, but if you desire marriage, you should seek God's wisdom and counsel through godly people to keep you protected and on course.

If you want to get married, that should be your end goal, and you should make it clear at the beginning of a relationship. If a man tells you he does not want to be married (or married to you), he means it, and having sex with him is not going to change his mind. However, he will still gladly have sex with you and take anything else you're offering, if you allow it.

Therefore, wasting time in these situations will only set you up for a cycle of sexual sin and delay you from having the relationship/marriage you want. Remember, time is the one thing you can never get back, so use it wisely. While we all have the same standard of living righteously, God knows your past and what will be the best path for you when it comes to dating. However, I don't think it is wise to date for an extended period without an end goal.

The devil desires to keep us away from the truth at all costs, so he will continue to sell you the lie that what you are doing now is better than what God has to offer. How could it be better when we can clearly see the consequences of not following God's plan? Children born out of wedlock, children fathered by multiple men, unhealthy relationships, and emotional and physical trauma—does this sound like a better way?

To sum up, boyfriend/girlfriend relationships distract you from becoming a wife. Instead, they keep you focused on being someone's Boo or Bae and set you up for a cycle of sexual immorality. On the other hand, courtship with the intent to marry or remain single and celibate are behaviors that will guard you and keep you on the righteous path.

Daughter, if you choose to believe the lie of the enemy, you will continue in relationships based on your selfish desires over God's plan. This only furthers the enemy's plan, assuring that generation after generation will become more committed to being uncommitted.

Prayer

God, please expose any lies I have believed about boyfriends, dating, and sex that are contrary to the truth of Your word. Open my eyes, ears, and heart to receive the truth of Your word and the wisdom to apply it to my life. In Jesus' name, Amen.

Chapter 2
DO YOU REMEMBER YOUR FIRST TIME?

"I heard you were a virgin!"

Yelled one of my male classmates in the middle of typing class (he will remain nameless to protect the innocent). I was in high school, and I think he was trying to embarrass me. But I wasn't embarrassed at all because, before my "first time," I was quite proud of the fact that I was a virgin. So, I politely responded, "Yes, I am."

Virgin: a person who has not had sexual intercourse; an unmarried girl or woman; chaste – fresh, unspoiled specifically: not altered by human activity.

I am not even sure if the word "virgin" is still in circulation today. Since the rise of feminism and the sexual revolution, if you said you were a virgin, you would probably be considered a unicorn. So, for the record, a virgin is a woman who has never had sexual intercourse, and that used to be regarded as a good thing. So, where did we get the idea that it wasn't?

The Feminist Movement

At the heart of the feminist movement that began in the 1970s was the idea that, apart from the right to have careers, women also have sexual needs and enjoy sex as much as men. Once women saw themselves on an equal playing field with men, sexual relations were no longer reserved for marriage or procreation. Thus, women felt free to have sex as much as they wanted, with as many men as they desired, because, in their minds, that made them equal to men. This fight for sexual equality also championed the use of contraceptives (the pill) and abortion. Feminists saw this as a victory because they could do as they pleased without the commitment or pressure of being a wife or mother.

This celebration of social and sexual liberation welcomed the single life, free love, one-night stands, friends with benefits, and hookup culture. As a result, fewer women became interested in maintaining their virginity and pursuing the role of wife and mother. Instead, they began to explore careers outside the home, choosing college and career over marriage. Fewer women were getting married because the one thing men wanted (and were willing to marry for) was sex. But now that women were so "liberated," men were getting sex freely without commitment.

So, instead of marriages and healthy families, we see an uptick in fatherlessness, single-parent homes, an increase in daycare and after-school care, abortion, low-income families, singleness, a decrease in marriages, a rise in divorces, and an increase in sexual partners—or, as it is referred to today, "your body count." Not only that, women's determination to be equal to men resulted in generations of proud feminist women who are mannish and aggressive, becoming everything but feminine.

In a nutshell, this is what happens when women want a sexual revolution. Interestingly, the word "revolution" implies rebellion, so the sexual revolution was a sexual rebellion against traditional norms and values.

What does God say about rebellion?

For rebellion is as the sin of witchcraft, and stubbornness is as iniquity and idolatry. Because thou hast rejected the word of the LORD, he hath also rejected thee from being king (1 Samuel 15:23).

In this passage of scripture, King Saul rebelled against the specific instructions of God to slay the Amalekites, their king, and all their livestock because he thought his way of doing things (i.e., sparing the king's life and the choicest flocks for an offering to God) was better than God's. That is why God disowned him as king.

Saul's rebellion is likened to witchcraft because, at the heart of witchcraft, is manipulation and control. He didn't want to be told what to do, so he thought he could appease God by partial obedience, which is still disobedience. Our choice to be sexually liberated is our way of telling God that we don't want to be told what to do. Then, when the relationships don't work, we try to manipulate God by crying, vowing never to do it again, or blaming someone else for our misfortune.

Fighting for sexual freedoms and equality with men has caused women to be deceived, just like Eve, into believing that God was keeping something from us when He gave us boundaries. So, the enemy tells us we have the right to do whatever men do under the slogan "My body, my right." In other words, you can be a god—the same lie he sold to Eve.

> *And the serpent said unto the woman, Ye shall not surely die: For God doth know that in the day ye eat thereof, then your eyes shall be opened, and ye shall be as gods, knowing good and evil.* (Genesis 3:5)`

Unfortunately, women are now feeling the effects of what happens when you believe the lie. We see women in their 30s, 40s, and 50s who have achieved wealth and success but have never been married, are childless, or have children out of wedlock. Many are now discovering that they have rebelled against the very thing they were created for: family. Sadly, the fight for equality became a forfeiture of purpose for those women who passed on the opportunity of marriage and family in exchange for sexual deviance and material gain.

And for the record, God never said women weren't equal to men. However, He did create different roles and responsibilities for men and women, and made our bodies and temperaments complement each other, which maintains balance in a relationship.

This is why God established clear boundaries in His word for sexual purity. The sexual relationship is to be kept between one man and one woman who have committed themselves to each other through marriage. Anything outside of this commitment constitutes sexual sin and will be judged as such.

> *Marriage is honorable in all, and the bed undefiled: but whoremongers and adulterers God will judge* (Hebrews 13:4).

This sexual revolution produced a decline in morality and an increase in sexual promiscuity and selfishness. We now consider being single, serial dating, and casual sex societal norms, but they are judgments resulting from rebellion.

Do you know that, of all sins, sexual sin acts against our own bodies? That's why 1 Corinthians 6:18 urges us: "*Flee fornication. Every sin that a man doeth is without the body; but he that committeth fornication sinneth against his own body.*"

Our lives were designed to reflect the image and plan of God. But if you believe you no longer need to remain sexually pure until marriage, then there is no purpose for your virginity, and you will discard your treasure as if it were trash.

Just think about this paradox: Today, we are encouraged to save the planet! We are told that eating organic, using non-toxic products, and recycling are helpful to us and our environment. But why don't we take that same stance when it comes to keeping our bodies pure or saving our virginity? How absurd is it to go vegan because it's healthier for your body, while at the same time being sexually promiscuous, giving no thought to what multiple sex partners do to the body and mind?

Pop Culture

I can remember, in one of the episodes of *Living Single* (90s TV), ironically called "Virgin Territory," one of the women is concerned about having sex with her boyfriend because he is a virgin, and she is not. As she asks her friends for advice on what to do, the women begin to share their own "first-time" sexual experiences.

One by one, they casually begin to divulge the awkward circumstances of how they lost their virginity. This included having sex while watching a movie, the night before the prom, and in a bunk bed. We have seen scenes like this played out in what is known as coming-of-age movies (*Love and Basketball*, *ATL*, and *The Wood*). These movies depict awkward teenagers losing their virginity as an innocent, fun, and natural experience. This type of programming played a huge role in shaping how we felt about our sexuality, normalizing the idea that we were supposed to lose our virginity, explore our sexuality, and live recklessly in our teenage years.

Because many of us didn't have meaningful conversations about sex with our parents, aside from "Don't do it," "Use a condom," or "Don't get pregnant," music, movies, TV, and sometimes our peers became our source of sex education. On the surface, these shows seem to create solidarity among women, promoting a sense of sisterhood based on shared experience and empowerment through sexual exploration. But what these programs are really doing is promoting sexual promiscuity (under the guise of sexual freedom) and unhealthy, uncommitted relationships between men and women.

This is why our culture promotes sharing your first-time sexual experience as something to be worn like a badge of honor, rather than the life-changing event that it is. The plain truth is that a first-time sexual experience is an initiation rite into adulthood, where our innocence is stripped away.

Initiation rite: an act or ritual that a person must perform to be officially recognized as having joined a group or organization or as achieving a new status (such as adulthood).

This initiation is the starting point for how you see yourself sexually and how you engage in sexual intercourse from that point on. Chances are, if your "first time" did not occur within the marriage covenant, you have adopted a worldview where you don't see a problem with having sex outside of marriage. It's likely that you will continue down this path of having sex without being married or even seeing the need for marriage.

That is because this type of first-time experience initiates you into a path of promiscuity, in other words, having multiple sex partners. It's a path that detours you from all righteous routes.

Consider the sisterhood you are now initiated into: a group of single women sharing memories of their first-time experience, but not many—if any—are married to their "first." Without being brought into the light of the truth, it's only a matter of time before you're off on the next sexual experience, and then the next. As a result, sexual experiences outside of marriage become our new normal, and in retrospect, shows like *Living Single* taught us how to live single.

In summary, feminism, culture, and entertainment taught us to devalue our purity, and in doing so, devalue ourselves.

But there is value in being chaste (pure, unblemished, and unsullied). Someone who has never been involved in sexual sin does not need to fear sexually transmitted diseases, unwanted pregnancy, or endure the physical and psychological pain that accompanies these devastating consequences. Neither do you have to stress about being ghosted, becoming a single parent, having children fathered by multiple men, or running into past sexual partners and the shame of knowing this person has seen you naked.

My earnest plea is that you keep yourself pure and abstain from sex if you are not married, or, as my daughter likes to say, "Rest your front" (your vagina). Doing so will keep the pieces of your body, mind, and soul intact.

That said, I must ask: Do you remember your first time?

I don't have to know you or your background to know that you absolutely remember your first sexual encounter. Do you know how I know? Because it was designed to be that way.

In Genesis chapter 2, when God presents the woman to Adam, he immediately knows she was created for him. He recognizes that she is a part of his very being and that he can relate to her in a way that honors God. At that time, there was only one choice for Adam and that was the woman, Eve. The physical, spiritual, emotional, and sexual experiences they shared would be their first, and there would be nothing or no one else to compare it to. And that's exactly how God designed it to be: one man fully committed to one woman, with no second or third experience with another person—only a first and only.

Our virginity was never designed to be a casual memory in a string of multiple sexual experiences. It was supposed to be a cherished memory of the day we were initiated into womanhood with our husbands.

This is why understanding our purpose is important. We are not here to fumble through life and figure it out as we go. But if you don't know that you were created to reflect God's image, you will squander your time—and your body—on unrighteous deeds in the name of self-expression or so-called sexual liberation.

Now, while some of us went into our first sexual encounter willingly, I realize that many people did not. Unfortunately, because of the wickedness of mankind, some have experienced rape or molestation as a child or were improperly touched or exposed to sexual acts when they should not have been. Hideous acts like these are indications that the kingdom of darkness is at work. This was never God's plan for you, nor did you do anything to warrant such abuse; it is simply because people are sinful and choose to do bad things. Therefore, if you were violated in such a way, someone sinned against you.

This, unfortunately, is a traumatic first-time experience and can cause you to have a distorted view of sex. Troubling as they were, these occurrences can be dealt with through patience, forgiveness, and love—all of which God can use to heal your heart.

The good news is, whether you were a willing participant in your first sexual experience or were violated or exposed to sexual acts prematurely, God understands everything and has factored all these situations into His plan of restoration and healing for you. We will discuss this further in chapter 6.

My First Time

I well remember my "first time." I was sixteen years old, and I remember feeling such a deep longing to win the affection of this boy. Oddly enough, it wasn't a "physical" desire to be with him sexually as much as a longing for his acceptance. I was so overwhelmed with emotion and desperate for approval that I was willing to do anything to get it, even give up my virginity. And give it up, I did.

My mother always says it only takes one drink to become an alcoholic, one time getting high to become a drug addict, and only one time having sex to get pregnant—and that is exactly what happened to me. So, when I reminisce about my first time, I think of the shame I felt from being pregnant as a teenager, the stress of being ridiculed by my peers at school, and the rejection of the boy I had given up everything for.

Unfortunately, my life was starting to look like an episode of *Living Single*, but the difference was that their lives were scripted and supported by a laugh track.

On the other hand, I was suffering in real time, dealing with the consequences of my real-life decisions. While the cast of *Living Single* laughed their way through the stories of their "first time," I could never have been fully prepared for the years of bondage to sin that would be attached to mine.

Daughter, if you understand that your life is meant to reflect the image of God and that God created sexual intimacy for marriage, then your goal should be to remain pure until marriage. Thus, understanding the purpose of sex within marriage establishes the reason for purity.

Prayer

Father, please expose any thoughts I have about feminism, the sexual revolution, entertainment, and culture that have influenced my thinking or behavior. Reveal them to be lies, contrary to the truth of Your word. Open my eyes, ears, and heart to receive the truth of what Your word says about these things, and give me the wisdom and grace to align my thoughts and actions with Your word. In Jesus' name, Amen.

Chapter 3
LIETH AT THE DOOR

"Do you want me to come over?"

It was my boyfriend calling. I already knew what would happen, but at this point, I was in too deep, and I wasn't even trying to fight my flesh. So, I told him yes. At the time, I considered this behavior normal; he would call, we would get something to eat, then watch a movie at my home or his, alone, and then have sex.

Shortly after, I heard the knock at my door and, like always, I opened it. In my mind, I was just opening the door to my boyfriend, but I didn't know I was opening the door to much more.

> *If thou doest well, shalt thou not be accepted? and if thou doest not well, sin lieth at the door. And unto thee shall be his desire, and thou shalt rule over him (Genesis 4:7).*

In this passage of Scripture, God is speaking with Cain, who is upset that his offering was not accepted. God tells Cain that doing what is right will gain him acceptance, but doing what is wrong will place him in the grasp of sin. He warns Cain that sin has the desire to control him, but he must overcome it.

Unfortunately, Cain did not rule over sin. Instead, he killed his brother and was exiled to live as a fugitive and a vagabond (Genesis 4:11-12). Like his parents, Adam and Eve, who went from living effortlessly in the Garden of Eden to working tirelessly outside of the garden (Genesis 3:23), Cain learned that sin has consequences.

What were some of these consequences?

> *And the LORD God called unto Adam, and said unto him, Where art thou?* (Genesis 3:9).

Up until this point, Adam had known the joy of living in the presence of God from the moment he was created. Now, for the first time in his life, he is confronted with feelings he has never experienced before—feelings of fear and shame. If only he could turn back the hands of time, he would not be experiencing these emotions. But it's too late; the deed has been done, and God is calling for His creation.

So where is Adam? This once-perfect man and his wife are hiding behind some trees in the garden, afraid they will be found... naked! A far cry from where they started:

> *And they were both naked, the man and his wife, and were not ashamed* (Genesis 2:25).

What could cause two people who were once naked and unashamed to suddenly be naked and ashamed? One word:

SIN. Sin is a game-changer. And that's exactly what it did—it changed the game ... for everybody!

Genesis 3:1-5:

*Now the serpent was more subtil than any beast of the field which the L*ORD *God had made. And he said unto the woman, Yea, hath God said, Ye shall not eat of every tree of the garden? And the woman said unto the serpent, We may eat of the fruit of the trees of the garden: But of the fruit of the tree which is in the midst of the garden, God hath said, Ye shall not eat of it, neither shall ye touch it, lest ye die. And the serpent said unto the woman, Ye shall not surely die: For God doth know that in the day ye eat thereof, then your eyes shall be opened, and ye shall be as gods, knowing good and evil.*

Twisted in nature and true to form, the devil embodies the serpent to lure the woman into questioning God's intentions. Once he gets the woman into a dialogue, she is no match for him. He successfully gets her to doubt God's intentions and despise the role God created for her.

Enticed by the promise of being like God, the woman bought the lie, ate the fruit of the Tree of the Knowledge of Good and Evil, and then gave some to her husband. Immediately, their eyes were opened to the enormity of what they had done (Genesis 3:6-7). And just like that, sin and death entered the world through one man, Adam. Therefore, everyone born of the seed of Adam was born in sin and consequently sentenced to death.

Wherefore, as by one man sin entered into the world, and death by sin; and so death passed upon all men, for that all have sinned...
(Romans 5:12)

What Is Sin?

Sin means to miss the mark (miss the target, go astray, err) or to fall short of the standard God has established. 1 John 5:17 equates sin with unrighteousness: *"All unrighteousness is sin."* Because God is the creator of everything, He alone sets the standard for right and wrong. Therefore, everything must be measured against His righteousness.

What the serpent introduced in the garden was a knowledge that offers another way of living, one that does not need to be measured against God's standard and righteousness. In this way, you don't have to submit to God, because you are a god unto yourself (Genesis 3:5).

So, instead of trusting God, you "trust yourself" or "follow your heart." You decide what is right based on what you think is right because it's "your truth," but this is a lie. The truth? We are flawed because of sin, so what we believe is right is often far from it.

Proverbs 14:12 warns, *"There is a way which seemeth right unto a man, but the end thereof are the ways of death."*

Another way to look at sin is as rebellion or transgression, which is a revolt against the rules set by God. This is different from merely missing the mark or going the wrong way; it is a deliberate rebellion against the standards of God. It means transgressing or pushing past the boundaries that have been set. This happens when we know the difference between right and wrong, and we know what we are doing is wrong, but we choose to do it anyway. *"Therefore to him that knoweth to do good, and doeth it not, to him it is sin"* (James 4:17).

We can see the progression of what happens when we sin. First, we miss "the way," causing us to take the wrong path or do wrong, thus incurring guilt or shame for the wrong we have done and then forfeiting what God had planned for us. Then, we rebel or deliberately go against God's commands. Rebellion against the parameters that God has established—for whatever reason, whether cultural norms, societal influences, traditions, personal desires, etc.—is still rebellion. Therefore, anything that causes you to miss the standard God has established is sin.

Open Doors

There are multiple ways you can open the door to sin. The lust of the flesh, the lust of the eyes, and the pride of life are the avenues the enemy will typically target. It's the same tactic the serpent used against Eve in the Garden of Eden, and it will work on us if we have issues in any of these areas.

> *For all that is in the world, the lust of the flesh, and the lust of the eyes, and the pride of life, is not of the Father, but is of the world* (1 John 2:16).

That is why we are told to crucify our flesh and all its appetites because if the enemy can find an unresolved issue in our lives, he will use it against us (Galatians 5:24; Galatians 5:19-21).

The goal of the enemy is to arouse your senses in one of these areas: your flesh or your sensual appetites, your eyes or your desires, and being prideful about life. These gateways can lead you down paths that take you away from God.

The devil will use anything and everything to get you to open the door to sin so that he and his demonic family can access your life. "Access" means you have agreed to give him the power to be your influence or guide and to afflict or harass you. It's like the old Dracula movies—according to legend, the vampire could not enter your home without an invitation because a spiritual barrier blocked the doorway, which could only be breached by an invitation.

There is a basis of truth to this. Doors serve as barriers to entrance: an open door gives access, and a closed door prevents it. Sin breaches the spiritual barrier of safety that God provides and creates an opening for the enemy to come in—but he needs an invitation. When you decide to have sex outside the boundaries of marriage, you are agreeing with the family of darkness that you don't have to follow God's plan. Your agreement is the invitation that opens the door to the dark side.

Once the door is open, sin traps you like a net; its fabric of deception is woven and twisted together, making it extremely difficult to escape once you are in. And then, it starts to change you.

You see, once you open the door, you have no control over what comes in. That's how sin works. One moment of so-called pleasure can invite all kinds of lustful acts, leading you to do things you vowed you would never do.

That is the power of sin. It pays a wage for all its willing workers, and that wage is death.

Romans 6:20-23:

For when ye were the servants of sin, ye were free from righteousness. What fruit had ye then in those things whereof ye are now ashamed? for the end of those things is death. But now being made free from sin, and become servants to God, ye have your fruit unto holiness, and the end everlasting life. For the wages of sin is death; but the gift of God is eternal life through Jesus Christ our Lord.

God is standing and knocking at the door of your heart, patiently waiting for you to open it so that He can give you a new life:

"*Behold, I stand at the door, and knock: if any man hear my voice, and open the door, I will come in to him, and will sup with him, and he with me*" (Revelation 3:20).

As for me, I did not realize it at the time, but every time I had sex with my boyfriend, I was opening the door for the devil to have direct access to afflict my life. My rebellion was altering my course and leading me further away from God.

Daughter, the enemy of your soul is waiting at the door for you to open it so that he can bring destruction into your life. Therefore, be sober, vigilant, and mindful, as Apostle Peter said:

*Be sober, be vigilant; because your adversary the devil, as a roaring lion, walketh about, seeking whom he may devour … (*1 Peter 5:8)

Prayer

Father, please open my eyes, ears, and heart to receive the truth of Your Word concerning sin and sexual sin. Show me the sinful areas of my life that have offended You. Forgive me, and teach me to live righteously according to Your Word. In Jesus' name, Amen.

Chapter 4
LET'S TALK ABOUT SEX

"Lord, please forgive me."

As I walked my boyfriend to the door and kissed him goodnight, I couldn't help but wonder how in the world this happened again. It felt like I was stuck in a cycle of sex, repent, press repeat. Even though I had promised myself I was not going to give in to temptation, here I was again, taking that familiar walk of shame to fall on my knees and ask for God's forgiveness.

What is Sex?

The word "sex" is a biological term used to describe a male or female based on their reproductive organs. Over time, it has come to denote sexual intercourse. Sexual intercourse, or coitus, is a heterosexual reproductive act involving the penetration of the vagina by the penis. It is the physical union of male and female genitalia, accompanied by rhythmic movements.

Today, our society has tried to complicate things concerning sex and gender, but God made it very clear in His creation story what He created:

So God created man in his own image, in the image of God created he him; male and female created he them (Genesis 1:27).

In our world, sexual experience is sold as a rite of passage. The message of sexual liberation is to "explore with confidence," "It's your thing; do what you want to do," and the ever-popular "Everybody's doing it."

Sex has been marketed and weaponized by men and women alike. It has been used as a form of control, abuse, criminal enterprise, and the satisfaction of selfish desires. But that is not why it was created. Our bodies were created by God to bring honor to Him, not for sexually immoral acts.

Meats for the belly, and the belly for meats: but God shall destroy both it and them. Now the body is not for fornication, but for the Lord; and the Lord for the body (1 Corinthians 6:13).

Sexual intimacy is God's creation. As the Creator of life itself, God has the blueprint for how to enjoy life and the things He created. One of the gifts He gave us to enjoy is sexual intimacy, but only within the confines of a marriage relationship.

*And Adam **knew** Eve his wife; and she conceived, and bare Cain, and said, I have gotten a man from the LORD* (Genesis 4:1, emphasis added).

Sexual intimacy is how two people become one flesh. The term "know" used in "*Adam **knew** Eve*" is from the Hebrew root word *yada*. *Yada* is the same word used in "Know the LORD" (Jeremiah 31:34), which speaks of deep intimacy. Knowing goes beyond the physical; it is an emotional and spiritual bond with our spouse. Our body parts fit perfectly together because it is a union of one flesh to another, but it is also a union of hearts and minds.

God created sexual intimacy primarily for union and pleasure, and then for procreation, so that we would "be fruitful and multiply" on the earth, have children, and raise families. In all, God created sexual intimacy to reflect His goodness, and we do so when it is done the right way.

So, what happens when it is done the wrong way? Sexual intimacy then becomes sexual immorality, or sexual sin.

Sexual Sin

For the record, the Bible refers to sexual sin as sexual immorality or fornication. For consistency, I will refer to it as "sexual sin" from here on.

Earlier, we saw that sin is to miss the mark (standard) or to transgress the laws God has set in rebellion against Him. Sexual sin is a combination of both: you use your body for an unrighteous act; the act itself constitutes rebellion and causes you to miss God's standard.

In 1 Corinthians 6:18, we are warned to "*Flee fornication.*"

Fornication: voluntary sexual intercourse between two unmarried persons or two persons not married to each other. In the Bible, it's idolatry.

The Greek word for "fornication" is *porneia*, from which we get the word "pornography." Contrary to popular belief, the

Bible gives a clear definition of sexual sin as: Adultery and Fornication (Hebrews 13:4); Homosexuality (Leviticus 18:22; Romans 1:26-27), and even Bestiality (Leviticus 18:23). All these aberrations are the handiwork of the devil. He takes what God creates and distorts it from its original intent. So, instead of sex according to its intended design between a man and a woman, we see same-sex marriages, orgies, polygamy, polyamory, and the like. All these acts are perversions.

It is a perversion of identity when men act like women and vice versa. It is a perversion of who God created us to be and does not reflect His image accurately. God does not make mistakes; He created us in His image as male and female. Anything else is a perversion of the truth.

Sexual sin is the ultimate expression of a lack of identity and purpose. Why? Because everything God created has a purpose, including sex. If you don't understand the purpose for which something is created, you will misuse it. When we engage in sex without being married or with a person of the same gender, we lack an understanding of what our bodies were created for, or, even worse, we simply don't care.

And for those who claim they have a right to their own body, know that God, the Creator, thinks differently.

> *Know ye not that your bodies are the members of Christ? shall I then take the members of Christ, and make them the members of an harlot? God forbid. What? know ye not that he which is joined to an harlot is one body? for two, saith he, shall be one flesh. But he that is joined unto the Lord is one spirit.*

> *Flee fornication. Every sin that a man doeth is without the body; but he that committeth fornication sinneth against his own body. What? know ye not that your body is the temple of the Holy*

Ghost which is in you, which ye have of God, and ye are not your own? For ye are bought with a price: therefore glorify God in your body, and in your spirit, which are God's (1 Corinthians 6:15-20).

Our bodies serve as temples of the Holy Spirit. Therefore, using our bodies to commit sexual sin violates not only our bodies but also God's design for sex, the marriage covenant, and the Holy Spirit. What an insult to the Holy Spirit within us—He is dragged into the bed of fornication with us!

It's either "My Body, My Choice" or denying yourself and following Christ, but you can't do both.

And he said to them all, If any man will come after me, let him deny himself, and take up his cross daily, and follow me (Luke 9:23).

Ungodly Covenants

God knew that we would have sexual desires because He created sex for us. So, He allowed sex within the marriage covenant so that all sexual desires could be explored and shared in a safe place between two people.

On the flip side, when you have sex outside of marriage, the same rules apply.

Or do you not know that he who is joined to a prostitute becomes one body with her? For, as it is written, "The two will become one flesh" (1 Corinthians 6:16 ESV).

Sex outside of marriage still creates a covenant, but an ungodly one, because you are joining your body with another person and sharing a bond designed for marriage. When we allow any man who is not our husband to deposit his seed (DNA) inside of us, we degrade our bodies and our womb, which is meant to be a pure place to nourish the seed that produces children. Likewise, men who drop their seed (DNA) anywhere and everywhere lack understanding and disregard the purpose of creating a family and a legacy for themselves.

Even if you don't have children, you are still receiving deposits of DNA from different men. While contraceptives (condoms, the pill) may protect you from STDs or pregnancy, they will not protect you from the emotional and spiritual bondage created from this ungodly covenant.

What many people do not realize is that when an ungodly covenant is created between sexual partners, it allows spirits of fear, depression, rejection, suicide, and many personality disorders to afflict you. A woman who has had many sexual partners may wonder why she is driven toward strange sexual behaviors—it is because she has opened herself to foreign entities through intercourse.

After so many of these unholy covenants, not only does your body become fragmented, but your mind becomes fragmented as well. You give away parts of yourself to so many partners, and this fragmentation can lead to an increase in mental health issues. We have made so many of these covenants through bad decisions that our minds are becoming unstable because we were never created to be sexually intimate with more than one person.

Temple Worshipers

In biblical times, the pagan nations were known to worship many false gods, most notably Baal and Ashtoreth, the god and goddess of fertility. To appease these false gods, not only was perverted sexual behavior encouraged, but child sacrifice was often demanded.

> *And the children of Israel did evil in the sight of the LORD, and served Baalim: they forsook the LORD God of their fathers, which brought them out of the land of Egypt, and followed other gods, of the gods of the people that were round about them, and bowed themselves unto them, and provoked the LORD to anger. And they forsook the LORD, and served Baal and Ashtaroth* (Judges 2:11-13).

God warned the children of Israel not to follow the worship practices of the pagan nations because their idolatry and perverse, immoral practices were detestable to Him. God gave Israel instructions on what constituted acceptable worship to Him and warned them what would happen if they turned their hearts away from Him to worship false gods.

Idolatry: the worship of a physical object as a god, or the immoderate attachment, and devotion to something.

Idolatry is the worship of an idol or false god. Idols can be anything—a person, a worldview, material possessions, or even sex. Anything you put in the place of God is an idol. Sexual sin is like idolatry because both are forms of false god worship, with the god, in this case, being self. It makes you choose yourself—your desires, your dreams—over everyone, including God.

So, when you continue to sin sexually, you are choosing to please your flesh over what you know is right. In doing this, you replace God as Lord and make yourself a god.

Sexual intercourse is a covenant act of worship because our bodies are the temples we use to worship. When you have sex within the God-ordained covenant of marriage, you are covenanted under God and to your spouse, and this constitutes worship to God. However, when you have sex outside of marriage, you are still using your body as a temple of worship, but you are now covenanted to the kingdom of darkness, creating an unholy covenant with the person you are having sex with. As a result, the enemy gains access to afflict, possess, oppress, and wreak havoc in your life based on this one immoral act.

This is often why you can't stop having sex even when you decide not to—because you have made covenants through sexual sin that bind you to the very act.

> *Do you not know that if you present yourselves to anyone as obedient slaves, you are slaves of the one whom you obey, either of sin, which leads to death, or of obedience, which leads to righteousness?* (Romans 6:16 ESV)

One of the rituals of the pagan nations was to have male and female prostitutes who would perform sexual acts with worshipers to gain favor or blessings from their gods. When you engage in sexual sin, your temple is defiled, and you enter into idol worship, just like the pagans. The only difference is that you don't go to a physical temple to worship; instead, you use your body, which is a temple of God, to perform illicit sexual acts, thereby desecrating your temple (1 Corinthians 6:19, 3:16).

In the same manner, your bed (or wherever you choose to perform the illicit act) becomes your altar, and your body becomes the sacrifice. Then you prepare yourself for the ritual: showering, freshening up your hair and makeup, spraying perfume, dressing in sexy lingerie, and setting the mood by dimming the lights, lighting candles, burning incense, and turning on seductive music. You worship yourself as a goddess or diva (as we like to say) out of lust and create an ungodly covenant with the person you are having sex with. This constitutes worship of the devil and is a sin against God.

When we step outside the bounds of what God has ordained as acceptable worship, we cross over into pagan ritualistic worship, just as the Israelites did. In essence, we become temple prostitutes, thinking we can use our bodies as a way to appease the god of self, at the expense of others. Having sex for favors—designer handbags, clothes, rent, money, etc.—is no different from prostitution, and it is a selfish act. This is why we are told to flee fornication and idolatry!

Anything that leads you away from God will only lead you into bondage. Israel spent seventy years in captivity because of their idolatry. How many years have you been in captivity to the physical and emotional bondage of sexual sin?

Sex Sells

Have you ever wondered why we need to see a half-naked person to buy food, perfume, clothes, or anything else? It's because advertisers know that sex sells. But what is sex really selling? An image.

Remember the image you were created in:

So God created man in his own image, in the image of God created he him; male and female created he them (Genesis 1:27).

God's creation of man in His image and likeness gave man his identity. So, the devil must do one of two things: either get you to hate the image of God in which you were created or prevent you from seeing it at all. This results in one of the two sins we discussed earlier—sin by way of error by wandering away from God, or sin by rebellion.

For the devil to change our identity, he must present another image for us to desire to reflect. That's what sexual sin sells—another image in opposition to God's.

For instance, God created the woman as a helper to the man, to be protected and covered by him. The serpent deceived her into thinking that she didn't need God or the man to cover her and that she could take care of herself. When the serpent convinced her to eat the fruit, she disobeyed both her husband and God and became the first independent woman.

Similarly, the devil must get us to reject God's image, so he places another image before us to emulate. The independent woman, the "Boss," the promiscuous woman, and the feminist are all offensive to God because that is not what He created. He created the woman as a helpmate for her husband, chaste with a meek and quiet spirit, not loud and domineering (1 Peter 3:3-4). By contrast, the image of the modern woman, and even celebrity women, is aggressive, provocatively dressed, foul-mouthed, and mannish. When we celebrate these images or adopt their style or behavior, we are subconsciously mirroring the demonic family of darkness. And, if we are not careful, we can cross the line from admiration to idolatry.

This is how the devil steals your worship away from the true and living God—he gives you something or someone else to worship. Ironically, anything you worship outside of God (including self-worship) is worship to the devil.

Let's look at what happened to King David when he succumbed to sexual sin:

2 Samuel 11:2-4:

And it came to pass in an evening tide, that David arose from off his bed, and walked upon the roof of the king's house: and from the roof he saw a woman washing herself; and the woman was very beautiful to look upon. And David sent and enquired after the woman. And one said, Is not this Bathsheba, the daughter of Eliam, the wife of Uriah the Hittite? And David sent messengers, and took her; and she came in unto him, and he lay with her; for she was purified from her uncleanness: and she returned unto her house.

David was the King of Israel. When he saw Bathsheba bathing on the rooftop, he was determined to have her for himself, so he summoned her, even though he already had multiple wives and knew that Bathsheba was married to Uriah.

When Bathsheba became pregnant from this encounter, to cover his sin, David brought Uriah home from the war in hopes that he would sleep with Bathsheba so he could pin the pregnancy on him (diabolical!). However, Uriah was so committed and loyal to David that he slept outside the king's house and never went home to his wife. So, David resorted to murder. He had Uriah placed on the front line of the battlefield so that he is sure to die in battle.

David was known as a man after God's own heart, but because of sexual sin, he progressed from being an adulterer to a murderer. Are you starting to get a picture of how sexual sin works? With each sexual act, you are degraded and robbed of your God-given qualities because you are moved a little further away from the image you were supposed to reflect.

The devil's long-term desire is to strip you of your purpose, identity, and individuality. If he can get you to assimilate into the culture, you will accept the images he presents to you. You will settle for a lesser version of who you were created to be, content to look or act like everyone else for the sake of belonging.

The Consequences of Sexual Sin

Galatians 6:7-8:

Do not be deceived: God is not mocked, for whatever one sows, that will he also reap. For the one who sows to his own flesh will from the flesh reap corruption, but the one who sows to the Spirit will from the Spirit reap eternal life.

This scripture clearly explains that those who live to satisfy their fleshly desires will reap a harvest of death and decay. Do not deceive yourself into thinking you will get up from your bed of lust unscathed. That is not how sin works. There are always consequences—here are just a few:

You will not enter the Kingdom of God

1 Corinthians 6:9:

Know ye not that the unrighteous shall not inherit the kingdom of God? Be not deceived: neither fornicators, nor idolaters, nor adulterers, nor effeminate, nor abusers of themselves with mankind Nor thieves, nor covetous nor drunkards, nor revilers, nor extortioners, shall inherit the kingdom of God.

Choosing to practice sexual sin is a choice you make to forfeit the kingdom of God. This is not God's desire for you. He desires that none perish but that all come to repentance (2 Peter 3:9); nevertheless, He still gives you the right to choose. And just because you have committed to having sex exclusively with one person (if they are not your spouse), it does not make you exempt. If our relationships do not align with God's revealed plan for marriage, then we are in rebellion. If our sin makes the list in 1 Corinthians 6:9, we will not inherit the kingdom of God. To think otherwise is to deceive ourselves.

Derailment of Destiny

Remember the story of Samson, the judge? Samson confided the secret of his strength to Delilah, the Philistine seductress, who then delivered him into the hands of her people. They enslaved Samson, gouging out his eyes and making a public spectacle of him. While God granted Samson one last feat of destroying the temple along with the crowd of Philistines, Samson died with them (Judges 16:1-31). Sex outside of marriage takes us out from under the protection of God's plan and purpose for us, leaving us wide open to attacks from the enemy. That's exactly what happened to Samson: the judge became the one judged.

Like Samson, we forfeit God's plan for our lives because sin takes us off the righteous path. In His mercy, God may still use us for His purpose, but sometimes we forfeit His plan for us altogether.

"Sexual sin causes you to take detours in life, where you waste time, and eventually run into a dead end. The enemy likes it this way because it keeps you trapped in a cycle of sin, making you unfit to be used by God.

The Ripple Effect

Back to David. Not only did he resort to murder to cover his adulterous affair, but his sin affected the lives of so many others. Bathsheba's husband, Uriah, was killed in battle, and Bathsheba became both an adulteress and a widow. The baby born out of the affair died soon after birth. David would now have trouble in his household forever, with incidents of rape, incest, and murder among his children (2 Samuel 12:1-14). All of this occurred because of sexual sin.

We may think our sin is a private matter involving only two people, but this is a lie. Every decision we make always affects someone else. For example, if you have a child out of wedlock, that child may have to deal with being raised by a single parent or having their life divided between two parents, which can create feelings of rejection and instability. Remember, one moment of sinful pleasure can change the course of our lives and the lives of those around us.

False Bonds

Earlier in this chapter, we saw how God created marriage to be a safe place where two people could become one and bring honor to God; this is a true bond. However, when we join our flesh with someone outside of the marriage covenant, we create a false bond, and a false bond leads to bondage.

There are instances in the Bible of the act of a person joining themselves to another person through sexual sin, creating a false bond, with dire consequences.

Dinah and Shechem (Genesis 34:2-4): Shechem, the son of Hamor, lusted after Dinah, the daughter of Jacob. He forced himself on her sexually, which made his soul long for her, so he decided to make her his wife. But Jacob's sons were angry that Shechem had defiled their sister, so they made a fake peace settlement, where they consented to intermarriage between the two groups on the condition that the men of the city of Hamor be circumcised. While the men were recovering from their circumcision, Jacob's sons, Simeon and Levi, along with a company of men slew all the men and plundered the city, bringing shame to Jacob.

Amnon and Tamar (2 Samuel 13:1-39): Amnon desired his half-sister Tamar so much that he pretended to be ill and had her bring food to him and feed him. Once they were alone, he tried to persuade her to lie with him. When she refused to engage in such a wicked act, he raped her. Immediately afterward, his desire for her turned to hatred. He refused to marry her to cover her disgrace and threw her out of his house. As a result, Tamar's brother Absalom waited patiently for two years until he had the opportunity to take revenge and have Amnon killed.

In both stories, the actions of these men ended in tragedy for many innocent people because they acted on their lustful desires (James 1:14-15). Their actions were not based on truth and honor but on lies and impure motives. Their emotional ties to these women created a false bond or ungodly covenant.

When we pursue sexually immoral relationships outside the boundaries God has provided, we develop emotional and physical ties that will always produce unfavorable outcomes.

Emotional Trauma

It goes without saying that when we enter into any relationship, we develop emotional attachments. However, ungodly covenants can keep us emotionally attached to some people even long after the relationship has ended. The emotional trauma from breakups can cause regret and shame, and if not resolved, these feelings can linger in our lives, and can cause us to be untrusting, detached, suspicious, and anxious toward others, making it impossible to have healthy relationships.

Fear and Shame

We've already discussed how Adam and his wife were naked and, in their innocence, unashamed. After they sinned, guilt caused them to realize they were naked and afraid (Genesis 3:10-11). Sin will always result in us feeling some form of fear or shame because sin violates the laws of God inherent in us. Sexual sin will ALWAYS produce feelings of shame because you violate your body.

Shame is to be embarrassed, humiliated, degraded, or disgraced. When you give your body to someone and are rejected, ghosted, catch an STD, get pregnant, or experience a breakup, this will result in feelings of shame, which can then lead to depression or other feelings of regret. We already saw from 1 Corinthians 6:18 how sexual immorality is a sin against your own body. Therefore, the consequences of sexual sin are no different. Because you use your body to sin, your body receives the consequences. This can change the course of your life, especially the course God had planned for you.

But look at what our society does. It mocks what God has created to be pleasurable and good within the confines of marriage and instead says sex should be casual and fun. They call it freedom of expression, women's liberation, and, worst of all, "love." But they never tell you about the loneliness, lack of fulfillment, heartbreak, or emptiness these types of relationships bring. Is this women's empowerment?

Daughter, when you listen to the enemy's lies, you trade the beauty of two becoming one flesh for the temporary pleasure of one person being known by many. God had a specific purpose for confining sexual intimacy to marriage, and God's plan will always be the best way. There is safety in this, as it keeps your mind and body whole.

Prayer

Father, forgive me for participating in sexually immoral acts. Please open my eyes, my ears, and my heart to understand Your purpose for sex and how my sexual sin has offended You. I know that there are consequences to my disobedience that I must endure, but I ask for Your mercy and grace as I take responsibility for my actions. Give me the mind and heart to receive the truth of Your word as it concerns sexual sin, and teach me how to live righteously according to Your word. In Jesus' name, Amen.

Chapter 5
VOWS, COVENANTS AND CURSES

"Why can't I get over him?"

It was the early '90s, and I was sitting in my car with the music blasting, singing loud and strong: "Since you've been gone, I've been hangin' around here lately with my mind messed up…" I was listening to *Another Sad Love Song* by Toni Braxton, my singer of choice for relationship therapy. To me, these lyrics were relevant and eased the pain of my broken heart. But could it be that these same lyrics were keeping me bound to the heartbreak and memories of my now ex-boyfriend?

A covenant is a solemn and binding agreement, usually instituted formally between two or more parties. In biblical times,

God used covenants to demonstrate the faithfulness of His character toward His people. These covenants contained promises for those faithful to the oath and were typically conditional: blessings for obedience and curses for disobedience.

God continually made covenants with man in the Old and New Testaments to show His desire to be involved in our lives. With Adam, He promised provision, prosperity, and dominion as long as he did not eat from that one tree (Genesis 1:28; 2:17). With Noah, He promised never to flood the earth again and sealed it with a rainbow (Genesis 9:1-16). Through Abraham, He said He would bless all the families of the earth that believed in Him through faith (Genesis 12:3). With Moses, He established the law so that God's people could be His special possession and prosper (Exodus 19:5). And with David, He promised an everlasting throne to the kingdom of Judah (Psalm 89:3-4).

This is the backdrop to the covenant of marriage. If we understand the depth of God's desire for intimacy with His people, we can appreciate how God uses the covenant of marriage as a living representation of His love for His body, the church. This is so profound that it remains a mystery (Ephesians 5:25-32)—a covenant so strong that a man would leave his father and mother to embrace his wife.

> Genesis 2:23:
>
> *And Adam said, This is now bone of my bones, and flesh of my flesh: she shall be called Woman, because she was taken out of Man. Therefore shall a man leave his father and his mother, and shall cleave unto his wife: and they shall be one flesh.*

When God formed the woman out of Adam's rib and brought her to Adam, he immediately recognized that she was organically a part of him and for him, and he called her "woman."

And just like that, they became husband and wife—no lavish ceremony, no bridesmaids or groomsmen, no cake and punch. Just one man who saw one woman and realized that he needed her to fulfill their God-given purpose together (Genesis 1:28).

So, the marriage covenant is an agreement made between one man and one woman before God, symbolizing the relationship of the church as the Bride of Christ and the Bridegroom, Jesus Christ (Ephesians 5:25–27). Thus, marriage is not only a physical but also a spiritual covenant.

Vows

To enact the covenant, vows are made by each individual, binding themselves to keep the conditions of the covenant.

A vow is a solemn promise or assertion—one by which a person is bound to an act, service, or condition.

Once the vows have been exchanged, the marriage covenant is solidified through the act of sexual intimacy. This covenant act completes the vows, whereby blood is exchanged, which is how the two become one flesh (mentally and physically). The Bible refers to it as *"knowing."*

"*And Adam **knew** Eve his wife; and she conceived, and bare Cain …*" (Genesis 4:1, emphasis added).

"Knowing" expresses physical, mental, and spiritual oneness that can only be understood in the context of two people who have committed themselves to each other and God in a covenantal relationship. It is the most intimate act where we are completely naked, vulnerable, and submitted to each other.

These are the blessings we receive from sexual intimacy in the marriage covenant:

The Blessing of Procreation (Genesis 1:28). God gave us the charge to multiply His creation by reproducing families who reflect His image. Our obedience in this brings God's glory to the earth and blessings to our families.

The Blessing of Covering. The husband, as the reflection of God the Father, covers the family.

The Blessing of Order and Identity (Genesis 2:23). While the husband is the head of the household, the wife, as a reflection of the Holy Spirit, comes alongside the man as a helper, submitted to his headship. (In our culture, this is symbolized by the woman taking the man's last name; they become one, and she is under his covering/name.) Thus, children are born with a name and family to which they can identify, and parents to whom they submit.

The Blessing of Honor (1 Corinthians 6:20). Sexual intimacy within marriage produces honor between the husband and wife, which brings honor to God.

The Blessing of Unity (1 Corinthians 7:3-5). As one flesh, sexual intimacy within marriage fosters physical, mental, and spiritual bonding between one man and one woman. Such unity produces strength and protects against the devil's attacks.

The Blessing of Provision (Genesis 1:28). Sexual intimacy within marriage enables the man to reflect the image of God as a provider. The man can provide for, protect, and lead his family in one household.

The Blessing of Pleasure (Proverbs 5:18-19). Everything that God created is with good intent; thus, sex is meant to be good and pleasurable for a husband and wife.

This is what God intended from the beginning, but now, because of sin, we know both good and evil. The introduction of evil in the world meant we would have to contend with curses.

Curses

In Jesus' confrontation with one of the seven churches in the book of Revelation, He specifically points to the sins of idolatry and fornication:

> *But I have a few things against thee, because thou hast there them that hold the doctrine of Balaam, who taught Balac to cast a stumbling block before the children of Israel, to eat things sacrificed unto idols, and to commit fornication* (Revelation 2:14).

Who was Balaam and what did he teach Balak? Balaam was a prophet who was solicited by Balak, the King of Moab, to curse the children of Israel, and was promised a huge reward for the job. However, Balaam made several attempts to curse the Israelites, but instead ended up pronouncing blessings on them each time because God would not allow him to curse them.

Still determined to get his reward, Balaam thought of a way for the children of Israel to curse themselves. He told the King of Moab to send Moabite women to the camp, who not only had sex with the men but also invited them to partake in their idolatrous feasts and bow to their gods. In doing so, the people yoked themselves to Baal of Peor. As a result, God sent a plague upon the children of Israel, killing twenty-four thousand (Numbers 25:1-2; 8-9).

The children of Israel had been protected and blessed by God because of their obedience, to the point where no one could curse them. But the moment they committed fornication, which led to idolatry, the protection of God was lifted, and the door was opened for them to be plagued by their enemies, both physically and spiritually.

The same rules apply to us today. When we follow the commandments of God, we are covered and protected; when we step outside His will, we are fair game for the enemy. The devil knows that he cannot curse you as long as you follow God's commands. However, he can get you to curse yourself by getting you to open the door to sin, especially sexual sin. Once those doors are opened, the devil has access to afflict your life.

Curse: words used to invoke a supernatural power to inflict punishment or harm on a person or thing.

Curses are the opposite of blessings. If blessings are the empowerment to prosper, then curses are the empowerment to fail. Whereas blessings bring life, joy, health, strength, growth, and prosperity, curses bring death, depression, sickness, anger, and poverty. Curses are consequences of disobedience to the Word of God. And because the devil is a cursed being, when you sin sexually, you enter into a covenant with him—knowingly or unknowingly—and are by default brought into the realm of curses (Jeremiah 17:5).

Therefore, all the blessings that are meant to be shared within marriage are reversed in sexual sin. The reversal of procreation is miscarriages and abortion; the reversal of marriage is divorce, separation, or the inability to marry; and the reversal of two-parent households is single-parent households.

The enemy does not tell you before you engage in sexual sin that you are making a covenant with the family of darkness. Any information he provides will be false; he only needs your agreement. Remember, the devil does not play fair. He wants you to make a covenant with him so that he can enter your life. He uses our immaturity, lack of knowledge, pride, and unresolved emotional or childhood trauma to get us to make vows that will keep us bound to ungodly relationships.

Vows made outside of a marriage covenant are just as binding as vows made within marriage. So, when you say things like, "I can't live without you," "I will never love anyone else but you," or "We will be together forever," these are vows. When you consummate the relationship with illicit sex, you have entered an unrighteous covenant.

Think of how many songs contain lyrics like: "I can't get you out of my head," "I'll die without you," "You're the center of my life," or "I can't breathe without you." We sing these songs when we're in love, and we sing these songs when we break up, not realizing that we are making a declaration—a vow, if you will. Then we wonder why we can't get that person out of our heads. It's because we made a vow not to. The enemy then moves in to afflict us with depression, loneliness, unforgiveness, or regret, trapping us in a cycle where we can't move on or trust again. All of these are spiritual ramifications of an ungodly sexual covenant.

That's why we are instructed in the Bible not to make vows randomly or carelessly, (even to God) (Ecclesiastes 5:4-8) or to swear an oath (Matthew 5:34-37), because doing so has the potential to bring us into bondage.

God's purpose for covenants stands because He is eternal. His purpose doesn't change just because we make a mistake. What He intended for the marriage covenant, including sex, applies regardless of whether or not you are married.

So, to sum up, sexual intimacy in marriage is:

- An act of obedience
- An act of submission
- An act of worship
- An act of sacrifice
- An act of love
- An act of trust
- An act of commitment
- An act of freedom

Sex outside of marriage is:

- An act of rebellion
- An act of idolatry
- An act of perversion
- An act of fear
- An act of bondage
- An act of humiliation
- An act of selfishness
- An act of the flesh

If you believe in the blessing, you have to believe in the curse because it is the antithesis of blessing.

God's way will always bring blessings because He is love, life, and blessings. But when you agree with the devil, you will get what he is—evil, lies, and curses. Under God's covenant, there is protection. When you come out from under His protection, you are walking in disobedience, and legally, the devil has the right to afflict you because you are walking in his territory. In God's covenant, you are empowered to prosper; in the devil's covenant, you are empowered to fail because the ungodly covenant is not based on two people agreeing to commit, but rather on two people agreeing to join their lustful desires in sin. That's why these ungodly relationships never work: there is always fear, arguing, cheating, chaos, anger, or poverty. It's because the curse of disobedience is preventing you from prospering.

Therefore, ungodly covenants and vows must be acknowledged, repented of, and renounced so that we may close the door of access the devil has gained through our lack of knowledge or disobedience.

Daughter, remember God does not give us instructions for living because He is a controlling, overbearing Father, as the world would have you think. Just the opposite—He gives us instructions for living because He knows the enemy is waiting for us to cross the line. God never wants you to be unloved, harmed, or cursed, but again, He will not override your will and will allow you the freedom to choose whom you will serve.

Prayer

Father, reveal to me every ungodly covenant or vow that I entered into with the family of darkness, knowingly or unknowingly, because of my sexual sin. I repent of my involvement in these acts and ask that I be released from any curses that have come through the open door of sin. Please open my eyes, ears, and heart to receive the truth of Your word, and cleanse me from all unrighteousness. Forgive me for my sin, and teach me to live righteously according to Your word. In Jesus' name, Amen.

Chapter 6
LET THE HEALING BEGIN

"Lord, I want to be healed"

When I first began my journey to healing, I wasn't sure what was happening. I just remember that God slowly began to unpeel the layers of my wounded soul. Things I had forgotten in the past (or chosen not to remember)—bad decisions, painful memories, and hurtful words—had all become interwoven into the core of who I was. All of these things needed to be unraveled and resolved.

I was aware of my past transgressions, so I was prepared to be judged. Instead, God, in His mercy and grace, covered me with His love as He exposed my deep-seated wounds. So, instead of feeling condemned, I felt an overwhelming sense of love and comfort. No doubt, I had been a rebel against God; I had disobeyed His word and done a lot of dumb things. But none of this changed His love for me.

So, because God is love, even when He disciplines us, it is because He loves us.

> *"My son, do not regard lightly the discipline of the Lord, nor be weary when reproved by him. For the Lord disciplines the one he loves, and chastises every son whom he receives." God is treating you as sons. For what son is there whom his father does not discipline?* (Hebrews 12:5–7 ESV)

God loves because He is love (1 John 4:8). Therefore, our behavior or misbehavior does not determine His love for us.

This is the first lesson on your journey to healing: **God loves you**.

No doubt, if you have been involved in sexual sin, there is a sense of guilt and shame. You may feel that it is impossible for God to love you, but He can and He does. In fact, the reason He sent His Son, Jesus, to die for our sins is because He loved us so much. Remember, *"For God so loved the world …"* (John 3:16).

I can assure you that whatever you have done in your past, you will never escape the love of God. He knows everything about you.

Psalm 139:1-18 says it all:

1. *O Lord, thou hast searched me, and known me.*
2. *Thou knowest my downsitting and mine uprising, thou understandest my thought afar off.*
3. *Thou compassest my path and my lying down, and art acquainted with all my ways.*

4. *For there is not a word in my tongue, but, lo, O Lord, thou knowest it altogether.*

5. *Thou hast beset me behind and before, and laid thine hand upon me.*

6. *Such knowledge is too wonderful for me; it is high, I cannot attain unto it.*

7. *Whither shall I go from thy spirit? or whither shall I flee from thy presence?*

8. *If I ascend up into heaven, thou art there: if I make my bed in hell, behold, thou art there.*

9. *If I take the wings of the morning, and dwell in the uttermost parts of the sea;*

10. *Even there shall thy hand lead me, and thy right hand shall hold me.*

11. *If I say, Surely the darkness shall cover me; even the night shall be light about me.*

12. *Yea, the darkness hideth not from thee; but the night shineth as the day: the darkness and the light are both alike to thee.*

13. *For thou hast possessed my reins: thou hast covered me in my mother's womb.*

14. *I will praise thee; for I am fearfully and wonderfully made: marvellous are thy works; and that my soul knoweth right well.*

15. *My substance was not hid from thee, when I was made in secret, and curiously wrought in the lowest parts of the earth.*

16. *Thine eyes did see my substance, yet being unperfect; and in thy book all my members were written, which in continuance were fashioned, when as yet there was none of them.*

17. *How precious also are thy thoughts unto me, O God! how great is the sum of them!*
18. *If I should count them, they are more in number than the sand: when I awake, I am still with thee.*

This is one of the most beautiful psalms in the Bible. It reminds me that our lives (even the parts we try to hide) are fully exposed to God, and He still chooses to love us. And it's His unconditional love that helps us heal.

The second lesson in healing is: **You have been forgiven**.

This is the beauty of salvation and the hope in which we believe. God does not hold our sins against us; when we ask for forgiveness, He cleanses us from every stain that sin has left.

Come now, and let us reason together, saith the LORD: though your sins be as scarlet, they shall be as white as snow; though they be red like crimson, they shall be as wool (Isaiah 1:18).

When we repent of our sins and ask for God's forgiveness, we are forgiven, end of story. But most of the time, we keep the story going in our minds—we press the repeat button, rehearse our mistakes, and criticize and judge ourselves for our missteps, making it impossible to receive God's mercy and forgiveness.

This is condemnation, and the truth is that we are no longer condemned when we are in Christ (Romans 8:1). Condemnation and guilt come from the enemy to keep us in a state of regret. But we only need to confess our sin, turn from our sin, and receive God's cleansing and forgiveness (1 John 1:9). There is no need for begging for mercy, no lengthy prayers with false promises—simply repent and turn from your sin.

This is important to understand because, depending on what you did in your past, you may not believe or feel that you have been forgiven. You may think that your sins are unforgivable or that your life is not worth saving, but these are lies.

You may think, "You don't know what I've done." You're right, I don't—but God does, which is why He sent Jesus to pay the penalty for sin and death because He knew we couldn't. We only need to take God at His word and trust that when He says we are forgiven, we are forgiven and receive His peace through forgiveness. This is what we call believing by faith.

> ... *as far as the east is from the west, so far has he removed our transgressions from us* (Psalm 103:12 NIV).

The third lesson in healing is **Sanctification.**

Sanctification occurs after we are born again. It is the process of being purified through God's Word so that we may be remade into the image of Christ. This is a continuous process that will not be completed until the return of Jesus Christ. Philippians 1:6 tells us, "*Being confident of this very thing, that* He *which hath begun a good work in you will perform it until the day of Jesus Christ.*"

With that said, we will always be a work in progress, continually growing in our walk with Christ. And sanctification is the process that helps us grow. It is a work done by the Holy Spirit that changes us from the inside so that we reflect the image of God on the outside.

Through sanctification, we are cleansed of our sinful behaviors and destructive patterns of our old life and transformed, set apart to be used by God.

So, He patiently waits until He knows you are ready to deal with an issue. Then He reveals the truth about the issue and lovingly walks you through the process of being healed in that area (if you are willing to be healed).

In my case, God would shine His light on an issue in my life, and I would have to face it. Then He would gently show me what needed to be done to resolve the issue. It started with repentance, and from there, it could involve anything from throwing away old memorabilia (pictures of old boyfriends, gifts, jewelry, clothing, etc.) or music, to forgiving someone or going back to ask someone's forgiveness.

Now, let me caution you—this is not an easy process. The reason why we do not deal with most of our issues is that they are too painful. They bring up too many emotions, bad memories, and heartache, and it's much easier to tuck them away neatly where no one can see them. The only problem is that our issues aren't hidden; everyone can see them. They show up in the form of bad attitudes, outbursts of anger, trust issues, perfectionism, being bossy or controlling, overspending, and – you guessed it – sexual sin.

Most of the time, we try to justify this behavior under the heading, "This is just who I am," but that is not the true you. 2 Corinthians 5:17 tells us explicitly who we are:

> "*Therefore, if any man be in Christ, he is a new creature: old things are passed away; behold, all things are become new.*"

When we are born again, we are a new creation in Christ, so the things we used to do, we don't have to do anymore. And even though God can instantly heal you from your issues, for the most part, you will have to work through them. That is why it's so important to cooperate with the Holy Spirit to renew your mind through the Word of God.

Keep in mind that there are ugly things God may reveal from your past, but He doesn't bring these things up to condemn or judge you, because they are under the blood of Jesus once you repent.

However, He does reveal them to us to help us realize what we did wrong, so that we can be healed and avoid becoming entangled in them again.

> *For this is the will of God, even your sanctification, that ye should abstain from fornication: That every one of you should know how to possess his vessel in sanctification and honor…* (1 Thessalonians 4:3)

If you have ever wondered what God's will for your life is, it's sanctification. The process of sanctification includes:

Abstaining from Fornication

Sexual sin hinders the sanctification process and prevents us from properly reflecting the image of God. Abstaining from fornication ensures that we keep our lives clean and in fellowship with God.

Self-control

We are required to have control over our bodies. We are not to be reckless in our decisions or controlled by our passions. It is God's will that we are knowledgeable in how to keep ourselves holy in order to honor Him.

Remember, sanctification is a personal process between you and the God who knows and loves you. What I may have had to go through for healing may not be what you go through. Again, only God knows the journey you must take.

However, there are some common steps we all must take when it comes to our sanctification.

Prayer

1 John 5:14-15:

And this is the confidence that we have in him, that, if we ask any thing according to his will, he heareth us: And if we know that he hear us, whatsoever we ask, we know that we have the petitions that we desired of him.

Prayer is how we communicate with God. The Bible encourages us to always pray (Luke 18:1). Jesus prayed constantly (Luke 6:12, Mark 1:35), and He taught the disciples how to pray (Matthew 6:5-15).

Prayer is a vital part of our life as believers, and it is where we begin our healing process. Every other step of our healing process—repentance, forgiveness, revelation, and healing—will happen during our prayer time with God.

Confession

1 John 1:9:

If we confess our sins, he is faithful and just to forgive us our sins, and to cleanse us from all unrighteousness.

God is faithful to His word and faithful to us. The more time we spend with God, the more we learn to trust Him and not be afraid to confess when we have failed. Confessing our sins is the only way we can be forgiven and cleansed of them.

I am not talking about going to a confessional and telling your sins to a priest; we don't need a middleman. Our belief in Jesus as our mediator gives us direct access to God the Father.

> *For there is one God, and one mediator between God and men, the man Christ Jesus; who gave himself a ransom for all, to be testified in due time* (1 Timothy 2:5-6).

When we acknowledge we have sinned and resolve to abandon our sin, we receive the mercy of God. But if we try to cover our sins, we will forfeit God's mercy and we will not prosper.

> *Whoever conceals his transgressions will not prosper, but he who confesses and forsakes them will obtain mercy* (Proverbs 28:13 ESV).

Repentance

Repentance first occurs when we understand that we are sinful beings and accept Jesus as our Savior. We are then cleansed from every sin through the sacrificial blood of Jesus Christ, redeemed back to God, in right standing with Him, and no longer His enemy. However, repentance does not end there; it's a continual part of our sanctification as God begins to show us the depth of our sin and allows us to repent of our involvement.

True repentance comes with a brokenness that goes beyond apologizing for what you have done (and then doing it again) or feeling sorry because you got caught. True repentance occurs when you see your sin as God sees it, and it grieves you as much as it grieves Him. It is then that we are brought to a place of brokenness, with a desire to give up and turn completely away from the sinful behavior that has kept us distant from God. We need the help of the Holy Spirit to see ourselves in this way.

That's the definition of repentance: to be sorrowful, broken, and remorseful for your actions, and then *turn away* from such behavior. It comes from the Greek word *metanoia,* which means "changing one's mind." True repentance is the path to being changed and healed.

> *Repent ye therefore, and be converted, that your sins may be blotted out, when the times of refreshing shall come from the presence of the Lord* (Acts 3:19).

Finally, there is **Restoration**. To restore something is to bring it back to its original state, as if it were never broken. Only the power of God can remove the stain of perverse acts and dirty deeds done in our past, and put us back in a place as if it never happened. This is the beauty of the healing process.

Daughter, through God's grace, you will find acceptance and assurance that you are loved, forgiven, and, through sanctification, you can be healed and restored.

Prayer

Father, thank You for bringing me to a place of brokenness so that I may see my sexual sin as you see it. Thank you for showing me mercy, allowing me time to humble myself, and truly repent for offending You. Forgive me for violating Your commands. I have resolved to turn away from my sin and all persons and places associated with it. Thank You for Your forgiveness and love for me despite how much I hurt You. Thank You for strengthening me whenever I am tempted again. Thank you for your peace and healing, and for restoring my soul. In Jesus' name, Amen.

Chapter 7
LEARNING TO FORGIVE

"You got Daddy issues!"

It was in the middle of an intense discussion with my "boyfriend" at the time when he pointed out that I was emotionally disconnected because I had issues with my dad.

Well, that's dumb, I thought, because I hardly ever saw or talked to my dad, so what's he got to do with anything? Sadly, it wasn't until long after we broke up that I began to understand what he was saying. My "daddy issues" had created a void in my heart that I didn't even know existed. His absence left me wanting, which led me down a path of looking for love through male companionship. However, my lack of connection with my dad also made it difficult for me to connect with men emotionally.

I never felt like I was resentful towards my father, so I didn't see the need to forgive him. "Out of sight, out of mind" is what I always used to say. However, my resentment towards him was showing through my inability to have healthy relationships and – you guessed it – sexual sin.

Honor Your Parents

Ephesians 6:2 (ESV) tells us, *"Honor your father and mother" (this is the first commandment with a promise).*

In a perfect world, our earthly father's presence was to reflect the image of our heavenly Father. Thus, being able to love and trust our earthly father would have made it easy for us to love and trust God. However, in the real world, our parents are human beings with issues of their own. They've experienced heartbreak, disappointment, and probably a lot of other things we will never know. Because of their unresolved issues, many of us have grown up as children of divorce, in single-parent households, or as victims of abuse or neglect. This type of childhood trauma can make us critical of our parents.

Nevertheless, God instructed us to honor our parents, not because of what they did or did not do, but because He knows that we are all sinful human beings in need of a Savior: "For *all have sinned and come short of the glory of God…"* (Romans 3:23).

For this reason, God has offered salvation to us all through Jesus Christ. Once we are born again, we are forgiven of all our sins (Ephesians 1:7). Therefore, we must forgive others, no matter how many times they wrong us.

> *Then Peter came to Him and said, "Lord, how often shall my brother sin against me, and I forgive him? Up to seven times?"*

Jesus said to him, "I do not say to you, up to seven times, but up to seventy times seven" (Matthew 18:21-22 NKJV).

Jesus uses this as an opportunity to tell a parable.

"Therefore the kingdom of heaven is like a certain king who wanted to settle accounts with his servants. And when he had begun to settle accounts, one was brought to him who owed him ten thousand talents. But as he was not able to pay, his master commanded that he be sold, with his wife and children and all that he had, and that payment be made. The servant therefore fell down before him, saying, 'Master, have patience with me, and I will pay you all.' Then the master of that servant was moved with compassion, released him, and forgave him the debt."

"But that servant went out and found one of his fellow servants who owed him a hundred denarii; and he laid hands on him and took him by the throat, saying, 'Pay me what you owe!' So his fellow servant fell down at his feet and begged him, saying, 'Have patience with me, and I will pay you all.' And he would not, but went and threw him into prison till he should pay the debt. So when his fellow servants saw what had been done, they were very grieved, and came and told their master all that had been done. Then his master, after he had called him, said to him, 'You wicked servant! I forgave you all that debt because you begged me. Should you not also have had compassion on your fellow servant, just as I had pity on you?' And his master was angry, and delivered him to the torturers until he should pay all that was due to him." (Matthew 18:23-35 NKJV).

Please look at the last verse: "... *And his master was angry, and delivered him to the torturers.*" Who, may I ask, are the torturers? I believe they refer to more than just jailers. They signify mental torture. The broader meaning is that when you hold unforgiveness in your heart, it leads to mental unrest, bitterness, anger, hatred, and thoughts of revenge. All this gives rise to many psychological and physical disorders, which can cause mental breakdowns and serious illnesses. Not to mention, unforgiveness keeps us in a place of stagnation, where we are unable to move on with our lives because we are bound to the offense.

God showed me that I too have offended, hurt, and disappointed others in my lifetime, and if I wanted to be forgiven for my sins, I was going to have to forgive others. That included my father.

So, I had to take an honest look at how I felt about my dad. I had to see him as a human being with flaws, and then I had to decide to release him from the debt I felt I was owed. Even today, I still have moments when I need to work through feelings or issues I have because of the lack of a relationship with my dad. Nevertheless, I have forgiven him.

It's best to seek the wisdom of God as it pertains to your relationship with your parents and how you interact with them. Relationships with parents can sometimes be toxic, but we must still honor them, and you can't honor your parents without forgiving them.

Honoring them means giving them respect because they gave you life. That doesn't mean you have to agree with everything they say or do, nor does it mean you have to subject yourself to abusive situations. It simply means being respectful to them. However, sometimes, to maintain peace, that must be done from afar. But forgiving them is non-negotiable: you must forgive to be forgiven.

For if ye forgive men their trespasses, your heavenly Father will also forgive you: But if ye forgive not men their trespasses, neither will your Father forgive your trespasses (Matthew 6:14-15).

Now, what does any of this have to do with sex? Our relationship with our parents can have a direct effect on how we process adult relationships. Traumatic childhood experiences cause us to develop unhealthy coping mechanisms, and that includes sexual relationships. Daddy issues can keep us searching for validation, and sex can be a way for us to feel loved and validated, even though sexual sin often produces the opposite—low self-worth, shame, and guilt.

That's why healing through forgiveness often begins with our parents. But it does not end there. You must follow the guidance of the Holy Spirit to lead you to the broken places in your life and expose the people you have not forgiven. Just because you don't interact with a person anymore does not mean you have forgiven them— that whole "out of sight, out of mind" approach won't work.

The truth is, during a breakup, you often walk away from the relationship leaving a piece of yourself behind, especially if you have been sexually involved. If the sexual sin has not been repented of, and you have not forgiven your ex, then you will carry those unresolved issues into the next relationship.

Forgiveness is crucial to your healing process. It is letting go of the offenses committed against you in exchange for the peace and healing of God.

Forgiveness is not justifying or approving what was done to you; it is simply choosing to live free from the bondage of anger, bitterness, and hate that holding on to the offense brings.

Forgiveness is giving up the right to avenge yourself of wrongdoing and trusting God to deal justly with the offender's consequences.

Finally, Jesus gave us the ultimate example of forgiveness:

> *And when they came to the place that is called The Skull, there they crucified him, and the criminals, one on his right and one on his left. And Jesus said, "Father, forgive them, for they know not what they do." And they cast lots to divide his garments* (Luke 23:33-34 ESV).

Daughter, Jesus was crucified for sins that He never committed—my sins, your sins, the whole world's sins. And in the middle of it all, He asked the Father to forgive those who were torturing Him. Are we better than Jesus? We are all guilty of sin; Jesus was guilty of nothing, yet paid the penalty for our sins. If He could forgive, we too can forgive.

Prayer

Father, forgive me for holding on to offenses and sins committed against me, and give me the heart to forgive as You have commanded. Please expose the people I have not forgiven, and give me the strength and courage to forgive them from my heart. Give me the grace to forgive my parents, and teach me how to honor them in a way that brings honor to You. Show me those I have offended and those from whom I need to ask for forgiveness. Open my eyes, ears, and heart to receive the truth of what Your word says about forgiveness, and give me the wisdom and grace to apply it to my life. In Jesus' name, Amen.

Chapter 8
CLOSING THE DOORS

"Who left the door open?"

We learned in Chapter 3 that doors serve as a barrier to an entrance, and that sin breaches that spiritual barrier and creates an opening for the enemy to come in.

Even though we are born again, we must be careful to repent of our participation in past sexual sins and deviant acts. Many believe that repentance is a one-and-done process, but repentance is a continual process in the life of a believer. Remember, sex is a covenantal act, so each time you have sex, you are making an ungodly covenant. For example, if you had five sexual partners, then five covenants were made. Therefore, you must repent of each covenant act of sin.

So, just because you break up with your boyfriend or even stop having sex does not mean you walk away free. I must reiterate that sexual sin breaches the boundaries of the spiritual realm, so even if you later marry the person you were having sex with, the first ungodly covenant still needs to be repented of.

> *I fear that when I come again my God may humble me before you, and I may have to mourn over many of those who sinned earlier and have not repented of the impurity, sexual immorality, and sensuality that they have practiced.* (2 Corinthians 12:21 ESV)

Therefore, when we are born again, God, in His mercy, begins walking us back through the trauma and sin in our lives so that we can repent and close the doors that were opened due to our disobedience.

How do we begin to undo what we cannot see in the spirit realm? Jesus, through the Holy Spirit, can help us go back into our past to those moments where sexual sin took place, and we must comply with what He instructs us to do.

We must acknowledge and confess our sinful acts to God, and by His Spirit, break all covenants we entered into with the kingdom of darkness.

This can be done through repentance, renunciation, and denunciation.

As we discussed earlier, repentance is a change of mind, where you see your sin as God sees it, and then turn completely away from it.

Renouncing is acknowledging that the things you participated in are evil and forsaking them. This includes the removal of any practices or paraphernalia you used that were tools of the enemy.

Denouncing is publicly declaring that you no longer agree with these evil deeds by speaking out against them or warning others about them.

This can only be done with the help of the Holy Spirit. He is the Spirit of Truth, and He will show you the truth about your sexual sin and the specifics of what you need to do to obtain deliverance.

In my case, what I had to do was write down the name of each person I had sex with, confess, and repent for the sexual sin in each case (1 John 1:9).

Then, I had to acknowledge and renounce each immoral act I had participated in, and denounce my affiliation with the kingdom of darkness, according to Jeremiah 3:13:

> *Only acknowledge thine iniquity, that thou hast transgressed against the LORD thy God, and hast scattered thy ways to the strangers under every green tree, and ye have not obeyed my voice, saith the Lord.*

Then I had to stop practicing sexual sin. I had to turn completely away from it.

I recommend this same process that God gave to me. However, it's best to seek the wisdom of God on how to deal with your past indiscretions.

Now let me be clear: just because you repent does not mean you won't have to suffer the consequences of your sin. Remember how David saw so much trouble in his family primarily because of his adultery? He repented for his sin, but he still had to suffer the consequences.

God is not mocked; you reap what you sow, and there are always consequences for disobeying God's commands (Galatians 6:7). However, God is merciful and gracious to us in that we don't always receive the judgments we deserve. God be praised!

Getting Rid of the Enemy's Things

Another way of keeping those doors open is by possessing things that belong to the family of darkness. Why? Because the devil's kingdom is cursed, and when we hold onto his possessions, we are holding onto cursed things.

This is how you can be born again but still struggle with sexual sins or demonic influences—because you are holding onto an accursed thing, and it is causing you to lose the battle against the enemy.

In the early church, when the people heard the gospel being preached, they believed, repented, and renounced and denounced their evil deeds. Those who had participated in witchcraft brought their books and materials and burned them openly.

> *Many who had believed now came forward, confessing and disclosing their deeds. And a number of those who had practiced magic arts brought their books and burned them in front of everyone. When the value of the books was calculated, the total came to fifty thousand drachmas. So the word of the Lord powerfully continued to spread and prevail ...* (Acts 19:18-20 BSB, emphasis added)

Likewise, we must take inventory of things in our homes or hearts that belong to the enemy. Then, we must be willing to purge them, no matter how much they cost. Pictures or gifts from old boyfriends, jewelry, music collections, clothing—all of these things represent a point of contact or agreement with a sinful act. As long as you keep them, the devil can still have access to you, even if it is just through holding onto memories.

Also, when the people confessed their deeds and burned their paraphernalia, the word of the Lord began to spread and prevail. Our attachments to things that belong to the kingdom of darkness prevent the power of God from working in our lives and hinder the testimony of Jesus. Remember, two families are at work here, and the family you agree with is the family that will prevail in your life and your children's lives.

The Spirit vs. The Flesh

Galatians 5:16-17

This I say then, Walk in the Spirit, and ye shall not fulfill the lust of the flesh. For the flesh lusteth against the Spirit, and the Spirit against the flesh: and these are contrary the one to the other: so that ye cannot do the things that ye would.

The *flesh* symbolizes our earthly, sensual human nature, which, apart from God, is inclined to sin.

We are encouraged to walk in the Spirit, and doing so will keep us from fulfilling the lusts of our flesh. Notwithstanding, our flesh is constantly in opposition to the Spirit. Even though we are born again, we must still contend with our flesh.

Galatians 5:22-23 gives a clear picture of what it looks like to walk in the Spirit:

But the fruit of the Spirit is love, joy, peace, longsuffering, gentleness, goodness, faith, Meekness, temperance: against such there is no law.

In contrast, we also see what it looks like to walk in the flesh.

Galatians 5:19-21:

Now the works of the flesh are manifest, which are these; Adultery, fornication, uncleanness, lasciviousness, Idolatry, witchcraft, hatred, variance, emulations, wrath, strife, seditions, heresies, Envyings, murders, drunkenness, revellings, and such like: of the which I tell you before, as I have also told you in time past, that they which do such things shall not inherit the kingdom of God.

Sexual sin is a work of the flesh. I have provided a list of practices related to sexual sin, based on the works of the flesh listed in Galatians 5. I will expound on some more than others, but keep in mind that this list is not exhaustive. Many other things can be added, so just because you don't see your particular sin, all of these things still need to be repented of, renounced, and denounced.

Adultery/Fornication

Ephesians 5:3–5

But fornication, and all uncleanness, or covetousness, let it not be once named among you, as becometh saints; Neither filthiness, nor foolish talking, nor jesting, which are not convenient: but rather giving of thanks. For this ye know, that no whoremonger, nor unclean person, nor covetous man, who is an idolater, hath any inheritance in the kingdom of Christ and of God.

Adultery is sexual intercourse between a married person and another person they are not married to.

Bestiality is sexual relations between a human being and an animal; it can also refer to displaying bestial traits or acting on animal-like impulses (Leviticus 20:15-16).

Homosexuality/Lesbianism is same-sex attraction or sexual relations between two people of the same sex.

Fornication is consensual sexual intercourse between two people who are not married to each other.

Prostitution and Whoredom refer to offering sex in exchange for payment, such as money, clothes, jewelry, etc. Even if you are having sex because you are looking for love or companionship, it is still a form of prostitution because you are offering your body in exchange for something (Hosea 4:12 and 5:4).

Promiscuity is uncontrolled sexual behavior with numerous partners.

Pornography is the depiction of erotic behavior in pictures, movies, or books that is intended to cause sexual arousal.

Many studies prove the negative effects that pornography has on the mind and sexual behavior. Scenes in movies and television that show even brief nudity can defile our minds because they plant seeds and cause imaginations that can lead to lies and sin. Also, keep in mind that pornographic acts involve 2 or more people, so you are not only being aroused by the opposite sex but you are being aroused by the same sex—a subtle trick of the enemy to plant seeds of same-sex attraction.

It is a sin to look at the nakedness of another man or woman who is not your spouse (see Leviticus 20). God puts certain parameters in place because He knows the evil intentions of the enemy and the damage one moment of exposure can do to the soul.

Molestation is the sexual abuse or assault of someone, especially a child. If you were violated sexually, doors were opened in the spirit for the enemy to torment you through depression, anger, unforgiveness, or more abuse. Ask God to give you the strength to forgive your offender and repent of any acts you adopted out of the abuse, such as promiscuity or anger. You are not responsible for being violated, but avoidance and unforgiveness keep the door open to evil attacks.

Perversion is sexually deviant behavior that is considered unnatural or abnormal. It is the destruction of something decent.

Sodomy is anal or oral intercourse with another person, particularly with a member of the same sex. It is also sexual intercourse between a human and an animal. Sodomy used to be considered "a crime against nature" and, until recent years, was considered an illegal activity. So, what changed to make it culturally accepted? Did God change His mind, or is it the wickedness of mankind?

Oral copulation/oral sex is sexual contact between the mouth of one person and the genitals or anus of another person, often referred to as fellatio, cunnilingus, or anilingus.

Again, this is another heavily debated topic. Many people do not view oral copulation as sex (copulation is another word for sex). It is defined as sodomy, a crime against nature because it goes against the act of procreation.

Uncleanness

2 Corinthians 6:17

Wherefore come out from among them, and be ye separate, saith the Lord, and touch not the unclean thing; and I will receive you.

Uncleanness refers to being dirty, filthy; morally or spiritually impure. This can also apply to physically keeping your body, house, or surroundings in an unclean state.

Profanity is the use of profane, obscene, or vulgar words specifically about sex or during sex.

Lasciviousness

Ephesians 4:19 (ESV)

They have become callous and have given themselves up to sensuality, greedy to practice every kind of impurity.

Lasciviousness refers to displaying behavior that is considered indecent or obscene or using your body as a sexual weapon to arouse others sexually.

Debauchery is extreme indulgence in bodily pleasures that are considered immoral, such as behavior involving drugs, sex, or alcohol.

Lewdness is obscene, vulgar, or crude comments, or sexually unchaste or shameless dress or behavior.

Spirit of Lust is intense sexual pleasure or unrestrained sexual desire, intended to create an intense longing or craving.

Hedonism is a doctrine that promotes pleasure or happiness as the greatest good in life, such as the idea to "Do what makes you feel good" or, according to occultist philosophy "Do what thou wilt."

Spirit of Seduction is using your body, attire, conversation, or actions with the intent to seduce, arouse, or tempt.

Idolatry

Psalms 135:15-18

The idols of the heathen are silver and gold, the work of men's hands. They have mouths, but they speak not; eyes have they, but they see not; They have ears, but they hear not; neither is there any breath in their mouths. They that make them are like unto them: so is every one that trusteth in them.

Yoga and Tantric Yoga – Yoga means "to yoke or join." Contrary to popular belief, yoga is not a form of exercise but a religion. The *asanas* or yoga poses are used to summon gods, and the breathing techniques and chants are meant to empty your mind so that you can be "enlightened," (or possessed), with the ultimate goal of becoming a god or one with the universe.

Tantric sex has the same goal of godhood and enlightenment but through sensual experiences, using breathing, meditation, and movement.

Sex Toys are any man-made devices or objects used to enhance sexual stimulation (such as vibrators, massagers, etc.).

One of the fruits of the Spirit is self-control (Galatians 5:23-24). We are instructed to know how to possess our bodies in an honorable way, set apart for God's use. That includes controlling your desires, particularly when they go against the word of God.

For this is the will of God, even your sanctification, that ye should abstain from fornication: That every one of you should know how to possess his vessel in sanctification and honor… (1 Thessalonians 4:3)

Sex toys require no self-control, which makes their use a work of the flesh. It is sexual immorality because it involves having sex with yourself, which is idolatry or self-worship.

Our culture promotes the use of sex toys as natural and empowering (you may even think this is a way of avoiding fornication or keeping your body count low). But remember, the family of light is truth, and everything in the family of darkness is falsehood, a lie, or a perversion of the truth. Sex toys, pornography, vibrators, etc., are all tools created by the family of darkness to show you how to pleasure yourself—it's a mind game.

Whatever sexual experiences you may have are not authentic if you are using man-made devices to pleasure yourself. Whatever thoughts or fantasies that occur during your experience are not real, and even if you reach a climax, it's a false experience because it's one you share with yourself.

Consider the spiritual ramifications. Sex, even with yourself, is a covenant act, so who is the covenant with? God created the marriage covenant between a man and a woman, so by default, a covenant outside of that is with the family of darkness. Therefore, demonic forces can stalk you, visit you in your dreams (having sex in your dreams, wet dreams), suggest evil sexual thoughts, cause you to fantasize about someone or something, or even cause insomnia or sleep paralysis because you have opened this door.

Do not be deceived—these toys are a subtle way of conditioning you to reject God and natural relationships as He intended, for self-indulgence. Thus, instead of seeking God to be content, waiting for a spouse, and having healthy relationships, you may say you don't need a man, yet satisfy yourself by choosing artificial stimulation over human touch. In short, you are choosing fantasy over truth, which is absurd.

Masturbation is the erotic stimulation of your own genitalia as a way to achieve sexual arousal.

This is one of the most debated topics, even in the church, so we will examine why it constitutes an open door to sin.

Our culture today will tell you that masturbation is totally normal and even healthy. So, why do so many people experience feelings of shame or guilt after they have masturbated? Could it be that this is not a natural function given to us by God?

God created man and woman to find pleasure in each other; that's why God said it is not good for man to be alone. Sexual intimacy is a journey of discovery that should be navigated between you and your spouse. Finding out what pleases each other strengthens communication, draws you closer, and allows for enjoyable intimacy.

Masturbation does the opposite: it lessens the need for companionship and supports the selfish nature. This can cause problems in marriage. Just think, if you have mastered self-pleasure, this could cause your spouse to feel inadequate because they are unable to arouse you.

Also, consider what masturbation does to the mind. It causes a retreat from reality, as you try to escape from the very purpose for which you were created.

Where does your mind go when you are masturbating? You must allow your mind to be taken to another place to arouse yourself, whether by focusing on pornographic images or visualizing yourself with someone you are not married to—this is a sin. Sexual fantasy, escapism, lust, visualization, vain imaginations, and perverse thoughts are all places you allow your mind to go to achieve sexual arousal for self-gratification.

The problem is that where your mind goes is likely to be in conflict with what God tells us to focus our minds upon:

> *Finally, brothers, whatever is true, whatever is honorable, whatever is just, whatever is pure, whatever is lovely, whatever is commendable, if there is any excellence, if there is anything worthy of praise, think about these things (*Philippians 4:8).

Can you honestly say that your mind goes to a pure or honest place when you are masturbating?

Again, this is a trick of the enemy to get you focused on self-pleasure through fantasy instead of trusting God for a real, lasting, and meaningful relationship with a spouse. Or instead of trusting God to be self-controlled and content through celibacy.

Witchcraft

Deuteronomy 18:10-11

> *There shall not be found among you any one that maketh his son or his daughter to pass through the fire, or that useth divination, or an observer of times, or an enchanter, or a witch, Or a charmer, or a consulter with familiar spirits, or a wizard, or a necromancer.*

Witchcraft is the use of sorcery or magic to try to attain a certain outcome. This includes communicating with the devil or demonic influences, consulting a familiar, a witch or psychic, tarot card readings, attending a séance, or practicing Wicca.

Amulets, Charms, and Stones – If you are using amulets, talismans, crystals, charms, stones, burning sage, incense, or candles to channel your sexual energy or harness sexual power, this is not of God; it is a form of witchcraft and must be repented of.

Astrology/Sexual Astrology involves the use of divination through the belief in the influence of stars and planets on human affairs and events.

Most people believe in astrology and faithfully follow horoscopes and zodiac signs. Astrology is defined as divination and is similar to observing the times, both of which are forbidden by God according to Deuteronomy 18:10-11. Furthermore, the definition of occult refers to magic, astrology, or any system claiming to use or have knowledge of secret or supernatural powers.

If you are consulting any supernatural power outside of God, like astrology, then you have another god, and you have forsaken the true and living God.

Numerology/Angel Numbers is the belief in occult, mystical, or divine relationships between numbers and events. Angel numbers are groups of repeating numbers believed to send messages from the spirit realm. Like astrology, this practice is forbidden. Using numerology to find or keep sexual partners is witchcraft and needs to be repented of.

Black Arts, Love Magic, or Sex Magic is any form of sexual activity used in spiritual or religious rituals that involve magic, spells, incantations, love potions, or hexes to win the affection of someone or keep them tied to you sexually.

Incantations and spells (roots, voodoo, hoodoo) - use of spells or verbal charms spoken or sung as part of a magic ritual;

a written or recited formula of words designed to produce a particular effect.

Manipulation/Destruction of Men

King Solomon was the wisest man who ever lived, but like the rest of the men of Israel, he was warned that intermarrying with women of pagan nations would turn his heart away from God.

> *1 Kings 11:3-5*
>
> *³ And he had seven hundred wives, princesses, and three hundred concubines: and his wives turned away his heart. ⁴ For it came to pass, when Solomon was old, that his wives turned away his heart after other gods: and his heart was not perfect with the Lord his God, as was the heart of David his father. ⁵ For Solomon went after Ashtoreth the goddess of the Zidonians, and after Milcom the abomination of the Ammonites.*

When we are sexually intimate with a man who is not our husband, we undermine his purpose, rob him of his strength, and turn his heart away from God because we contribute to him choosing sex with us over obedience to God (think Samson and Delilah).

Proverbs 6:26 warns of the danger of a promiscuous woman: *"For by means of a whorish woman a man is brought to a piece of bread: and the adulteress will hunt for the precious life."*

Our femininity can become a deadly weapon if used as a tool to seduce men. Many women say there are no good men (a lie) but continue having casual sex, stealing men's energy, and making them useless for the kingdom of God. Of course, men share in this responsibility, but we must take accountability for the wreckage of men we have left in our past. No wonder it's called your "body count."

Feminism is a movement that promotes sexual liberation and equality for women and fights against God's order.

Spirit of Jezebel/Baal worship Jezebel was a power-hungry Baal worshiper who sought to kill the prophets of God and destroy any man who would dare stand against her. She kept a host of eunuchs (castrated men) around her and dominated her dependent, weak husband, King Ahab.

This is a picture of the modern woman—the "Boss," "Queen," "Diva," or "Goddess"—career-driven, dominant, sexually aggressive, and out to gain as much money and power as she can. She doesn't need a man for procreation because she is not interested in it; neither does she need a man for pleasure because she has learned how to pleasure herself. If you have adopted this mindset, it needs to be repented of.

Hatred/Variance/Emulations/Wrath/Strife

Proverbs 29:22

An angry man stirreth up strife, and a furious man aboundeth in transgression.

James 3:16

For where envying and strife is, there is confusion and every evil work.

Spirit of Anger is seen through hostility or strife in a relationship, often holding on to unforgiveness (Ecclesiastes 7:9).

Contentiousness is being argumentative, quarrelsome, *aggressive,* belligerent, disagreeable, or showing hostile behavior (Proverbs 21:19).

Domestic abuse refers to personal relationships that result in violence or abuse. Repentance is needed here if you went into this relationship against the warnings of God, parents, friends, etc. (most of the time, there are red flags that we ignore). This door also needs to be closed because it can bring more abuse or even death. You will also have to ask God to give you a heart to forgive your abuser.

Divorce is the legal dissolution of a marriage.

Children born out of wedlock/single parenting result from babies being born to parents who are not married to each other.

Regardless of circumstances, children are a blessing from God (Psalm 127:3-5). However, single parenting is not a blessing, and in most cases, it is the result of sexual rebellion or disobedience. God never designed you to struggle financially or emotionally raising children alone. This is a consequence of having sex without being married (again, in most cases—there are exceptions).

Spirit of Fear/Compromise refers to compromising yourself sexually due to peer pressure or fear of losing a relationship.

Murder

Proverbs 6:16-17

These six things doth the LORD hate: yea, seven are an abomination unto him: A proud look, a lying tongue, and hands that shed innocent blood,

Abortion is a medical procedure used to terminate a pregnancy by removing the fetus.

Regardless of your view on abortion, the truth is that to abort a fetus before its time is to cause its death.

So, who gets to determine the value of a life? Is it you ("My body, my right") or God?

Consider the wisdom of Acts 17:24-26:

God that made the world and all things therein, seeing that he is Lord of heaven and earth, dwelleth not in temples made with hands; Neither is worshipped with men's hands, as though he needed any thing, seeing he giveth to all life, and breath, and all things; And hath made of one blood all nations of men for to dwell on all the face of the earth, and hath determined the times before appointed, and the bounds of their habitation;

God, the Creator of all things and the Giver of life to everything, is the only one qualified to determine the value of a life. God established the value of life when He created mankind in His image (Genesis 1:26) and commanded them to be fruitful and multiply (Genesis 1:28).

Abortion goes against the command of God to be fruitful and multiply and "thou shalt not kill" (Exodus 20:13). God gives life, while the enemy destroys.

The thief cometh not, but for to steal, and to kill, and to destroy: I am come that they might have life, and that they might have it more abundantly (John 10:10).

Molech was the god worshiped by the Ammonites and Phoenicians in biblical history. They sacrificed their children to this false god by burning them on altars of fire, believing that sacrificing their children would bring financial prosperity for their families and future children.

God forbade the children of Israel from participating in such heinous practices:

> *And thou shalt not let any of thy seed pass through the fire to Molech, neither shalt thou profane the name of thy God: I am the LORD* (Leviticus 18:21).

Abortion is a form of child sacrifice. Think about all the practical reasons women get abortions: they are not married, they are not financially stable, they want to pursue their career, they are not ready, they are too young, or they do not want children (in my case, I didn't want to have another child at that time). In all these instances (even my own), a child's life is sacrificed for the interests of the mother.

But the spiritual roots are deeper. Abortion is the strategy of the enemy to exterminate the family of God. You see, God gave us reproductive organs so that we could reproduce, create families, and thus build a legacy that reflects the righteous image of God.

Remember, God told the serpent that the woman's seed, Jesus, would ultimately destroy the seed of the enemy (Genesis 3:15). So, the enemy's goal has been to destroy the woman and her seed in an attempt to kill Jesus first, and then God's people:

- Pharoah attempts to kill all newborn boys at birth (Exodus 1:15-16).
- Herod attempts to kill the newborn Jesus by ordering the massacre of infants under two years old (Matthew 2:16).
- Today, we have abortion and the morning-after pill.

We can see from the above examples that the goal of the enemy is to reduce the number of those who will serve the true and living God and fight against the kingdom of darkness. When God says be fruitful, multiply, and replenish the earth, the devil says abort.

When you abort a baby, you assume the role of God and end the life of a child who had a destiny. Think of all the mighty men and women of the Bible, such as Moses and Samuel. Had they been aborted, they would not have been used by God, and we would not be reading about them today.

We need to recognize that the fight for reproductive rights is, in reality, a fight for the right to terminate rather than reproduce. Even organizations that claim to help you plan for parenthood often offer services to help you plan against it.

Abortion is another door that brings death and destruction into your life. It is a direct reflection of the enemy, who bears the image of death, whereas Jesus Christ brings life. Therefore, it must be repented of.

Drunkenness/Reveling (orgies, wild parties)

Proverbs 6:16-17

For the time that is past suffices for doing what the Gentiles want to do, living in sensuality, passions, drunkenness, orgies, drinking parties, and lawless idolatry.

Wild parties/College experiences include participating in sexually immoral acts, and rituals, taking oaths and vows, and making covenants as a pledge to Fraternities/Sororities/Freemasonry; or engaging in sexual experimentation or exploration.

This is considered a part of the "college experience," but it is wickedness and opens the door to promiscuity, heartbreak, and emotional trauma.

Orgies/threesomes/Swingers etc. are unrestrained sex parties where multiple people share in sexual activities. Again, this violates God's design for marriage: one man, one woman.

As I mentioned before, this list is not exhaustive. Just because you may not see something listed here does not mean it doesn't need to be repented of.

Also, if you don't agree with something listed here, I suggest asking God for understanding and clarity on the matter according to His word (Proverbs 3:5-6).

Daughter, I understand it may be tough to address or let go of some of these practices because you may enjoy doing them. But no one ever said sin wasn't pleasurable. Sin is enjoyable for a moment, but what it produces when it's finished is death. Anytime you are overtaken by a sin of any kind, you can expect the outcome to produce death or death-like consequences.

> *But each person is tempted when he is lured and enticed by his own desire. Then desire when it has conceived gives birth to sin, and sin when it is fully grown brings forth death* (James 1:14–15 ESV).

Prayer

Father, in the name of Jesus, I ask that You reveal to me by Your Holy Spirit every ungodly relationship and every door that was opened due to my sexual sin. I repent of my sexual sin with (name) and ask that You break all ties with this person—physically, spiritually, mentally, and emotionally.

I renounce every sexually immoral act that I participated in and every evil work that I committed or allowed into my life. I renounce any vows, covenants, and ungodly ties, and ask that I be cleansed from all unrighteousness according to 1 John 1:9-10.

I renounce every unclean thing I touched that opened the door to the enemy. I renounce and denounce acts of (list unclean things: abortion, masturbation, etc.).

I ask that the blood of Jesus wash me clean and release me from all judgments and curses brought into my life by the open door to sin.

I ask that the doors be closed and any curse be broken off of me and my children in the name of Jesus. Thank You for Your mercy and kindness. Amen.

Chapter 9
LIVING FREE

"Is that who I think it is?"

It was a pleasant afternoon, and our church was visiting another church for a conference when I noticed a familiar face in the crowd noticing me too. As he started walking across the room in my direction, I felt my heart beat faster.

We greeted each other and engaged in the usual small talk: "Good to see you!" "How is your family?" "What have you been up to?" Then he asked, "Do you want to grab something to eat?"

I stood there, staring, fumbling over what to say, and just before I could formulate a response, he said, "Wait here. I'll be right back," and walked away.

At that moment, I breathed a sigh of relief and calmed my nerves. Then I ran like my life depended on it! The odds were not in my favor—I was wearing high-heeled shoes and had parked down the street—but somehow, I managed to get down the street quickly without being noticed.

Why did I run? Because I saw my ex-boyfriend as a threat, emotionally and sexually. We had a history, and believe it or not, saying yes to one lunch date could potentially bring back a flood of memories (good or bad), including sexual ones. I'm not saying anything would have happened if I had gone out to lunch, but I wasn't interested in finding out.

God had delivered me from that relationship, and the peace I had come to know and the healing I had experienced were not worth giving up. I had been through enough to know that when God sets you free, you don't go back for lunch, dinner, coffee, or tea—you flee!

We see a biblical example of this in the story of Joseph in Genesis 39:1-23.

Joseph was a godly man with a strong prophetic calling, and he had just survived the unthinkable—being sold into slavery by his brothers.

His first stop was Potiphar's house, where he was put in charge of managing the household, which he did extremely well. It was clear that the favor of God was with Joseph, and everyone could see it, including Potiphar's wife. She pressed him every day, saying, "Lie with me," and every day, he refused. Joseph tried reasoning with her to get her to see that it would be dishonorable for him to betray her husband and, more importantly, to sin against God. But she wouldn't listen.

Finally, when no one was in the house, she made her move. She grabbed Joseph by his clothing and pressured him again, "Lie with me!" At that point, Joseph let his feet do the talking!

> *And it came to pass, as she spake to Joseph day by day, that he hearkened not unto her, to lie by her, or to be with her. And it came*

to pass about this time, that Joseph went into the house to do his business; and there was none of the men of the house there within. And she caught him by his garment, saying, Lie with me: and he left his garment in her hand, and fled, and got him out (Genesis 39:10).

Why didn't Joseph choose to indulge in sexual sin with Potiphar's wife? "Men will be men," right? Perhaps men who lack purpose and self-control, but Joseph lacked neither. God had given Joseph a dream, and although he may not have fully understood its meaning, he trusted God's plan. Had Joseph given in to her advances, it would have diverted his course and forfeited God's blessings.

Joseph ended up in prison because of Potiphar's wife's false accusations. However, because he chose to flee the temptation of sexual sin, he went to jail with his integrity intact, unscathed by sexual sin, and the Lord's favor remained with him.

This is what it looks like to live free from sexual sin—it's knowing God has a plan for your life and deciding that a few moments of pleasure are not worth losing what God has prepared for you. Living free from sexual sin will not be easy, but we have the help of the Holy Spirit, who can strengthen us. Nevertheless, we must be active participants in our deliverance.

Here are a few ways we can stay free.

Be Prepared to Stand

Ephesians 6:10-18 ESV:

Finally, be strong in the Lord and in the strength of his might. Put on the whole armor of God, that you may be able to stand against the schemes of the devil. For we do not wrestle against flesh and blood, but against the rulers, against the authorities, against the cosmic powers over this present darkness, against the spiritual forces of evil in the heavenly places. Therefore take up the whole armor of God, that you may be able to withstand in the evil day, and having done all, to stand firm. Stand therefore, having fastened on the belt of truth, and having put on the breastplate of righteousness, and, as shoes for your feet, having put on the readiness given by the gospel of peace. In all circumstances take up the shield of faith, with which you can extinguish all the flaming darts of the evil one; and take the helmet of salvation, and the sword of the Spirit, which is the word of God, praying at all times in the Spirit, with all prayer and supplication. To that end, keep alert with all perseverance, making supplication for all the saints ...

Do not think that the devil will just let you walk away freely to start serving God. Remember, our fight is not only physical but spiritual. Yes, there are practical things we can do to protect ourselves against the devil's attacks. We can avoid places of sin (even if it's aimlessly surfing the internet) or steer clear of people who are a source of temptation. But we must also be prepared spiritually. God has given us His armor for our protection: the belt of truth, the breastplate of righteousness, the shoes of the gospel of peace, the shield of faith, the helmet of salvation, and the sword of the Spirit—the word of God.

God is telling us who we are battling against, and the only way we can be protected is by standing against the enemy's attacks, fully suited in the armor and protection of God. If you fight in your flesh, you will lose.

We can also build up our character in the ways of God so that we have the mind of Christ. Let me offer a few safeguards.

Renew Your Mind

Romans 12:1

I beseech you therefore, brethren, by the mercies of God, that ye present your bodies a living sacrifice, holy, acceptable unto God, which is your reasonable service. And be not conformed to this world: but be ye transformed by the renewing of your mind, that ye may prove what is that good, and acceptable, and perfect, will of God.

When the children of Israel made their exodus out of Egypt, God had to begin the process of extracting Egypt from them. They had been enslaved by the Egyptians for so long that they had adopted many of their practices, including their practices of sin. Now that they were no longer prisoners of Pharaoh, God had to instruct them on what was acceptable worship to Him.

Likewise, God must show us a new way of living when we are born again because we cannot bring our old practices of sin into the kingdom of God. We learn this new way of living by staying connected to the word of God. It is His word that teaches us righteous ways, but it is our responsibility to read it and apply it to every area of our lives.

Keep Yourself Pure

2 Timothy 2:21

Therefore, if anyone cleanses himself from what is dishonorable, he will be a vessel for honorable use, set apart as holy, useful to the master of the house, ready for every good work. So flee youthful passions and pursue righteousness, faith, love, and peace, along with those who call on the Lord from a pure heart.

We have already established that sexual sin is dishonorable to ourselves, those we are involved with, and to God. Now that we know this, we are responsible for keeping ourselves pure from reckless and uncontrollable passions. Continued growth in our faith, knowledge, and relationship with Jesus Christ, along with the active pursuit of righteous living, will prevent us from making impulsive decisions (2 Peter 1:5-8; Philippians 4:8).

Remember, the Holy Spirit will assist and guide us, but He won't make us do anything. We must make a conscious decision to live differently and then make a conscious effort to do so. And just think—the payoff is huge, as we become a clean vessel that God can use to accomplish His good works.

Guard Your Heart

Proverbs 4:23

Keep thy heart with all diligence; for out of it are the issues of life.

You can be sexually stimulated by many things that come into your visual field. David was sexually stimulated by seeing a woman bathing to the extent that he sent his servants to inquire about her. However, he could have done one thing, and that is take his eyes (and mind) away from the object of his lust. It could have ended there and then. This is why you must be honest with yourself about your past sexual experiences, so you know the best way to guard yourself from falling into the same sinful patterns. Watch your emotions and be mindful of things that arouse you, then avoid them at all costs. It may be time to throw away those romance novels or turn off the TV.

Remember, you have an enemy who is always looking to gain a foothold in your life, and it's your job to ensure he doesn't. This is why we are told to crucify our flesh—because if there is some sin you are struggling with, the devil will find it and use it against you. *"And those who belong to Christ Jesus have crucified the flesh with its passions and desires"* (Galatians 5:24).

Avoid Evil

We are told in 1 Thessalonians 5:22, *"Abstain from all appearance of evil."*

What might the appearance of evil look like? This goes beyond running away when you are tempted by sexual sin; it applies to ALL appearances of evil. This can be very challenging in our world because many things we consider forms of entertainment are laced with subtle or blatant messages that undermine righteous living.

You may have to delete some of your social media accounts and old phone numbers or get a new number altogether. This may sound extreme, but staying free from sexual sin requires a sacrifice, and only you can decide what that freedom is worth to you.

Take Control of Your Thoughts

> 2 Corinthians 10:5 (ESV)
>
> *We destroy arguments and every lofty opinion raised against the knowledge of God, and take every thought captive to obey Christ,*

It is in our minds where the enemy does some of his best work. We are deceived into thinking that every thought in our head is ours, which makes the enemy so subtle in his deception. He will whisper in your ear: "God is mad at you," "No one will ever want you," "You are not good enough," "You are damaged goods," and the list— I mean lies—go on, because that's exactly what they are: lies!

When it comes to sexual sin, the enemy's goal is to draw you back into sin or make you feel guilty or ashamed of your past. Remember, guilt and shame separate you from God. The key is to remember that these are lies, and while you may have done those things in the past, you are now a new creation. Your past sins are under the blood of Jesus, and you have been forgiven.

Let me be clear: these are attacks of the enemy, and they need to be recognized and dealt with immediately. The way to deal with them is to reject and cast them down when they disagree with the word of God.

Thoughts are powerful. The longer you ponder a thought, the more it influences your behavior. So let us train our thoughts to focus on what's honest, lovely, and worthy of reflection, as in Philippians 4:8.

And when our thoughts are never far from God and His word, we have the assurance of His peace.

> *You will keep him in perfect peace whose mind is stayed on You, because he trusts in You* (Isaiah 26:3 (NKJV).

Watch What You Watch

Entertainment: the agreeable occupation for the mind; diversion; amusement

The word television itself says it all. It is telling you a vision. The question is, whose vision? If it goes against the standard of God, then you must ask yourself, Why is this entertaining to me?

Many TV shows today feature stylish and appealing women, yet they are often devoid of morality and portrayed as sex-crazed. This is an appearance of evil, so you should avoid watching such shows. Most movies are filled with violence, profanity, and— you guessed it— sex. Watching sexual scenes involving kissing or excessive touching has the potential to arouse your emotions or cause you to fantasize. Listening to sexually suggestive music can have an equally negative effect when you are trying to keep yourself pure.

Even music from "back in the day," which we tend to think is safe, should be reconsidered. Let me pull a few popular songs from different music eras, and note the song titles: *Let's Get It On* (Marvin Gaye), *Sex Machine* (James Brown), *Push It* (Salt and Peppa), *Little Red Corvette* (Prince), *Freak Me* (Silk), *Bump and Grind* (R. Kelly), *I Want To Sex You Up* (Color Me Badd), *Giving Him Something He Can Feel* (En Vogue), and *Anytime, Anyplace* (Janet Jackson). Dare I go on?

Songs from "Back in the Day" are especially dangerous because they can trigger emotions or memories from the past, so you may need to stop listening to such music.

Ask God for wisdom about what you should watch, read, and listen to. Romance novels, TV shows, and movies that promote sex, adultery, and lewd acts are not healthy ways to be entertained. Remember, the enemy will never give up on trying to draw you away from God's safety by getting you entangled in sin again.

And don't think it's a coincidence that you conveniently run into people from your past with whom you've been intimate, or someone who "remembers you when." These are strategic plans of the enemy to bring you back under the bondage of who you used to be. If you keep this in mind, you won't be fooled by random text messages, or thoughts and memories about past relationships.

Don't believe the lies

As you try to maintain your freedom from sexual sin, you will be tempted by culture, friends, or family with countless reasons why it's "natural" for you to give in to your sexual desires. But remember, this is just another trick of the enemy to get you off track and back into a cycle of sin. That is why staying grounded in the word of God is so important—if you don't know the truth, you will believe the lie.

Here are some lies about sex and the responses from the word of God.

1. "The Bible is outdated and doesn't apply to the issues of today."

   Ecclesiastes 1:9 NIV

   What has been will be again, what has been done will be done again; there is nothing new under the sun.

2. "Love is love" (it doesn't matter who you love).

   Romans 1:26-28

   For this cause God gave them up unto vile affections: for even their women did change the natural use into that which is against nature: And likewise also the men, leaving the natural use of the woman, burned in their lust one toward another; men with men working that which is unseemly, and receiving in themselves that recompence of their error which was meet. And even as they did not like to retain God in their knowledge, God gave them over to a reprobate mind, to do those things which are not convenient;

3. "Follow your heart" or "God knows my heart."

   Jeremiah 17:9

   The heart is deceitful above all things, and desperately wicked: who can know it?

   Jeremiah 17:5 NIV

   This is what the LORD says: "Cursed is the one who trusts in man, who draws strength from mere flesh and whose heart turns away from the LORD.

4. "I can do what I want to do."

   Galatians 6:7

   Be not deceived; God is not mocked: for whatsoever a man soweth, that shall he also reap.

   Galatians 6:8

   For he that soweth to his flesh shall of the flesh reap corruption; but he that soweth to the Spirit shall of the Spirit reap life everlasting.

5. "I am not hurting anyone if we both consent."

   Proverbs 21:2

   Every way of a man is right in his own eyes: but the LORD pondereth the hearts.

6. "You need to have sex before marriage to see if you are sexually compatible" (try before you buy)

   Proverbs 14:12

   There is a way which seemeth right unto a man, but the end thereof are the ways of death.

When we choose to practice sexual sin, we are rejecting the truth of God's word and choosing to believe a lie, which will lead to the consequences of that lie. However, when we choose to believe the truth about sex, we will make better choices by abstaining or waiting until we are married.

FLEE!

Flee - to flee away, seek safety by flight; to be saved by flight, to escape safely out of danger.

When it comes to sexual sin, we are given one instruction: flee. Not just walk away or say hi and bye – no, flee! Sex is the one battle God never tells us to fight because it's a battle we can't win. We are no match for our flesh, and once our flesh is aroused, it is next to impossible to get it unaroused.

> *For the flesh lusteth against the Spirit, and the Spirit against the flesh: and these are contrary the one to the other: so that ye cannot do the things that ye would* (Galatians 5:17).

You can have the best intentions, and you can be sincere in wanting to keep yourself from sexual sin. But if you have been feeding your flesh, it will be stronger than your spirit, and you will be overcome. That's why you must take every precaution to feed your Spirit with the word of God, prayer, and worship. This will help you grow strong in spirit and learn how to crucify your flesh.

Again, it is not wise to put yourself in situations where you will be tempted. Late-night phone calls (Booty Calls) and visits are not a good idea, especially if you have been involved in sexual sin before. You must be honest about your past sins so that you can guard yourself against future ones. Remember, abstinence does not mean deliverance—you may be abstaining simply because the opportunity to sin hasn't been presented.

> *No temptation has overtaken you that is not common to man. God is faithful, and he will not let you be tempted beyond your ability, but with the temptation, he will also provide the way of escape, that you may be able to endure it* (1 Corinthians 10:13 ESV).

Learn to be Content

This will probably be one of the most challenging areas in living free because loneliness and unfulfillment cause us to move faster than we should in many relationships.

> Philippians 4:11
>
> *I am not saying this out of need, for I have learned to be content regardless of my circumstances (BSB).*

Contentment is finding peace and purpose regardless of your circumstances. This means you can find pleasure in life without sex, without being in a relationship, and even without being married. Contentment comes from time spent with God and learning to trust and wait on His timing. The more time you spend in the presence of God, praying and reading His word, the more your so-called needs and desires begin to fade as God becomes your focus. In this space, you will realize that God is more than enough, and He places His desires for you in your heart.

> Psalm 37:4
>
> *Delight thyself also in the LORD; and he shall give thee the desires of thine heart.*

I know it sounds cliché, but you will grow to understand God's grace when you are tempted, His comfort when you are lonely, and His peace when you are anxious.

You can find contentment by serving others, such as caring for family members, visiting the elderly or sick, volunteering, getting involved in ministry at church, or participating in community service. Serving others helps take the focus off yourself and puts someone else's needs above your own, and you'd be surprised how much joy you find in doing so. This also teaches selflessness, a valuable character trait if you desire to be a wife.

I'm speaking from experience; it was contentment that kept me celibate and without dating for over 10 years. Although I desired marriage, I submitted to God, knowing that if it was not His plan for me, I would remain content to finish my course with Him alone. But God, in His love and kindness, granted me the joy of being a wife and blessed me with a wonderful husband.

Daughter, remember that temptation will come, but God, in His mercy, has provided layers of protection and guidance to keep you from falling into sexual sin. Through prayer, Bible study, and applying God's word in your practical life, you can avoid the enemy's tricks and ensure that you maintain your freedom.

You will find these scriptures on abstinence helpful:

Acts 15:20, Acts 15:29, Acts 21: 25, 1 Corinthians 10:8, 1 Thessalonians 4:3.

Prayer

Lord, You paid such a high price for my freedom, so let me walk in the freedom You gained for me. Let me be alert to all the occasions that will take me back to the sins of the past — the sights, the sounds, the smells, and tastes that my senses remember. Please help me be watchful and alert, especially with my entertainment choices. Holy Spirit, put a huge check in my heart when I carelessly wander into territory that will entice me to sin. Thank You for walking alongside me and guiding me. Amen.

Chapter 10
FINAL THOUGHTS

Daughter, life is about making choices and being mature enough to take responsibility for those choices, including the choices you've made about sex.

It may be difficult, but if you take an honest look at your past sexual relationships, you can see how those choices have affected the person you became. I say "the person you became" because you would probably have developed differently without making those choices. Still, they are your choices and part of your story—whether good, bad, or ugly. The real question is, "How do you want your story to end?"

Maybe you enjoy having sex and don't want to stop because, let's face it, sex is pleasurable. But let me remind you how the story ends for fornicators and adulterers.

> *Marriage is honourable in all, and the bed undefiled: but whoremongers and adulterers God will judge.* (Hebrews 13:4)
>
> *Know ye not that the unrighteous shall not inherit the kingdom of God? Be not deceived: neither fornicators, nor idolaters, nor*

adulterers, nor effeminate, nor abusers of themselves with mankind, Nor thieves, nor covetous, nor drunkards, nor revilers, nor extortioners, shall inherit the kingdom of God. (1 Corinthians 6:9-10)

Or perhaps you have done the unthinkable, the unforgivable. What if your body count is in double or even triple digits? What if you have a sexually transmitted disease? What if you are emotionally damaged? What if you have had one or multiple abortions? What if you have been molested or raped? What if you have children with different fathers? What if you have allowed yourself to be used and degraded? What if you think that no one will ever want you? Let me remind you how the story ends for those who put their hope in Jesus Christ.

But God showed his great love for us by sending Christ to die for us while we were still sinners. (Romans 5:8, NLT)

Therefore if any man be in Christ, he is a new creature: old things are passed away; behold, all things are become new. (2 Corinthians 5:17)

If we confess our sins, he is faithful and just to forgive us our sins, and to cleanse us from all unrighteousness. (1 John 1:9)

Come now, and let us reason together, saith the LORD: though your sins be as scarlet, they shall be as white as snow; though they be red like crimson, they shall be as wool. (Isaiah 1:18)

The good news is that your past does not determine your future, nor do your mistakes define who you can become through Jesus Christ. God is not surprised by the things you have done in your life—He knew everything about you before you were even born (read Psalm 139:1-18). Therefore, God does not rescue us because we are good; He rescues us because HE is good.

At the heart of the matter, we all want to be loved. The problem is, most, if not all of us, do not fully understand who love is:

> *Beloved, let us love one another: for love is of God; and everyone that loveth is born of God, and knoweth God. He that loveth not knoweth not God; for God is love. In this was manifested the love of God toward us, because that God sent his only begotten Son into the world, that we might live through him* (1 John 4:7-9).

Love is a Person, and that Person is God. If we do not accept this truth then we will never understand what love is:

> *Love is patient, love is kind. It does not envy, it does not boast, it is not proud. It does not dishonor others, it is not self-seeking, it is not easily angered, it keeps no record of wrongs. Love does not delight in evil but rejoices with the truth. It always protects, always trusts, always hopes, always perseveres* (1 Corinthians 13:4-7 NIV).

Sex is not love; God is love, and the only way we can know love is by knowing God. It's all a matter of choice.

God's way will always be the best choice, even though it is the road less traveled.

Matthew 7:13:

> *Enter ye in at the strait gate: for wide is the gate, and broad is the way, that leadeth to destruction, and many there be which go in thereat: Because strait is the gate, and narrow is the way, which leadeth unto life, and few there be that find it.*

Daughter, I pray that you choose to accept God's love and allow Him to cleanse you from the stain of sexual sin. I pray that you allow God to lift the burden of guilt and shame in exchange for His peace. I pray that you would allow God to heal you from your past, and trust Him with your future. I pray that you choose to be made whole in Jesus' name.

But the choice is still yours.

REFERENCES

"Virgin." Merriam-Webster.com Dictionary, Merriam-Webster, https://www.merriam-webster.com/dictionary/virgin. Accessed 26 Mar. 2024.

"Initiation rite." Merriam-Webster.com Dictionary, Merriam-Webster, https://www.merriam-webster.com/dictionary/initiation%20rite. Accessed 26 Mar. 2024.

"Astrology." Merriam-Webster.com Dictionary, Merriam-Webster, https://www.merriam-webster.com/dictionary/astrology. Accessed 3 Jun. 2024.

"Boyfriend." Merriam-Webster.com Dictionary, Merriam-Webster, https://www.merriam-webster.com/dictionary/boyfriend. Accessed 22 Jan. 2023.

https://www.pbs.org/wgbh/americanexperience/features/pill-and-sexual-revolution/

"Sexual intercourse." Merriam-Webster.com Dictionary, Merriam-Webster, https://www.merriam-webster.com/dictionary/sexual%20intercourse. Accessed 26 Mar. 2024.

"Vow." Merriam-Webster.com Dictionary, Merriam-Webster, https://www.merriam-webster.com/dictionary/vow. Accessed 30 Mar. 2024.

Worship." *Merriam-Webster.com Dictionary*, Merriam-Webster, https://www.merriam-webster.com/dictionary/worship. Accessed 6 Jan. 2021.

"Idolatry." *Merriam-Webster.com Dictionary*, Merriam-Webster, https://www.merriam-webster.com/dictionary/idolatry. Accessed 6 Jan. 2021.

"Fornication." *Dictionary.com*, Dictionary, https://www.dictionary.com/dictionary/idolatry. Accessed 6 Jan. 2021.

Content source: Division of STD Prevention, National Center for HIV/AIDS, viral Hepatitis, STD, and TB preventions, Centers for Disease Control and Prevention.

Centers for Disease Control and Prevention. Sexually Transmitted Disease Surveillance 2018. Atlanta: U.S. Department of Health and Human Services; 2019. DOI: 10.15620/cdc.79370

"Sex." Merriam-Webster.com Dictionary, Merriam-Webster, https://www.merriam-webster.com/dictionary/sex. Accessed 9 Jul. 2023.

"Virgin Territory." Living Single, Season 4, Episode 10.

"Death." Merriam-Webster.com Dictionary, Merriam-Webster, https://www.merriam-webster.com/dictionary/death. Accessed 4 Sep. 2023.

"Bondage." Merriam-Webster.com Dictionary, Merriam-Webster, https://www.merriam-webster.com/dictionary/bondage. Accessed 25 Jan. 2024.

https://www.who.int/news-room/fact-sheets/detail/abortion

https://www.yoga-society.com/blogs/types-of-yoga/tantric-yoga

www.ingramcontent.com/pod-product-compliance
Lightning Source LLC
Chambersburg PA
CBHW070636030426
42337CB00020B/4045